Published by Poppyland Publishing, North Walsham, Norfolk 1987.
Printed by Speedprint Design, Spalding, Lincolnshire.
Typeset by PTPS, Norwich.
Printed in Great Britain.

East Anglia

on Film

David Cleveland

A look at some of the films and film makers that have recorded the region's past, through films held in the East Anglian Film Archive at the University of East Anglia.

The East Anglian Film Archive

The East Anglian Film Archive, of which David Cleveland is Curator, is a collection of movie films and video tapes reflecting the history of the region and its people from the beginning of the present century until the present time. The aim of the Archive is to search out and preserve movie film of East Anglian content which show life and work in Norfolk, Suffolk, Essex and Cambridgeshire, and provide a service of access and presentation where copyright allows.

The Search for Film

The Archive is continually looking for film to add to the collection, either by donation or by borrowing and copying. Any film about the region, whether it is amateur or professional, may be of interest, no matter how old it is or what size film it is on.

Some 35mm film may be on celluloid or nitrate base. This type of film used in the cinema industry until about 1951 is highly inflammable and prone to rapid deterioration, which can destroy the image. When discovered, nitrate film should be examined and, if possible, copied without delay. 8mm, 9.5mm and 16mm are all on safety stock.

Films and Video Tapes

Master copies of most of the films are stored in air conditioned vaults to make sure the image is preserved for future generations. Viewing copies can be seen by appointment. The Archive publishes a catalogue of its holdings and some compilation video tapes are available for hire or purchase.

The new and the old. A television video crew filming - or should it be taping - a sequence in the film archive at the UEA.

Facilities at the Archive

The Film Archive produces catalogues of its holdings, and films and video tapes can be viewed on the premises by appointment for those studying and researching the region's history. Film presentations can be arranged for some of the material to schools, colleges, societies and clubs.

Housed in the Archive is a small museum of cine equipment. Cameras, projectors and associated items from 1899 to the 1970's help illustrate the history of cinematography.

The First Regional Film Archive

The East Anglian Film Archive, the first organised regional film archive in the country, was formed in the spring of 1976 as a joint venture between the University of Essex and the University of East Anglia. The Archive is housed in the Centre of East Anglian Studies at the University of East Anglia (Tel. Norwich 56161, ext. 2664) with a branch office at the University of Essex (Contact David Tilley, Colchester 873333) where copies of the Archive's catalogues can be inspected.

Contents

Acknowledgements

I am most grateful to Bob Malster for checking the following pages, and to Anthea Iveson for typing them. Nearly all the photographs are "blow-ups" from tiny frames of film - expertly done by Malcolm Howard, Jack Roberts and Paul Amos. Many thanks to those who have allowed me to reproduce these pictures.

Many friends and colleagues and film show audiences have given me much help and information, especially Don Chipperfield, Barrett Jenkins, Richard Rope, Peter Hawkins, E.W. Bostock, Peter Hollingham, Leslie Oakey, Michael Chalkley, Peter Boulton, Malcolm Freegard, June Lewis, David Tilley, Bernard Polley, Alan Wesencraft of the Harry Price Libary at London University, John Barnes of the Barnes Museum of Cinematography, and Miss Jean Kennedy and the staff of the Norfolk Record Office. Finally, my thanks to my wife Christine for all her help, particularly in checking through this text.

Introduction

I never cease to wonder at the invention of motion pictures. Photographs that moved, or animated photographs as they were known, were achieved in the last decade of Queen Victoria's reign, after much searching and experimentation by many people. The apparatus, the movie camera and projector, sometimes combined in a single machine, were purely mechanical - made of wood and brass, a formidable achievement.

Film is still with us today; the same gauge that William Dickson made for Edison in 1893 - 35mm - continues in our cinemas. A smaller gauge, 16mm, introduced in 1923, is used extensively in television, even in these days of video.

Much has been recorded - for that is what a movie camera is, a recording machine - and much has been lost, yet a good deal has survived in the non-fiction class and is stored safely in the country's archives. The National Film Archive does a magnificent job for the safe keeping of our national heritage and the smaller regional archives that sprang up in the 1970s save film of their own areas. The East Anglian Film Archive, now based at the Centre of East Anglian Studies at the University of East Anglia, was the first of these regional film archives and this book is based on films in this collection.

From this Archive it is possible to look at most aspects of life and work in Norfolk, Suffolk, Essex and Cambridgeshire, and also to glean a little film industry history.

Some of the films may seem quaint and in some cases poorly made and edited. These must be judged with the standards of the day in mind, and with background information to the type of film concerned. It is the content that is important, and that is why the East Anglian Film Archive is determined to preserve these old films for the enlightenment and entertainment of future generations.

This book and the Archive, with its hundreds of films on a wide range of subjects, would never have come into being were it not for all those film makers who have "exposed" film up and down East Anglia since 1896. It is to those people that it is dedicated.

D.C.

Early Days

As soon as movies burst upon the screen in 1895 the recording of everyday events began. In fact the first public film show in the world to have a paying audience, at the Grand Cafe in Paris on December 28th of that year, contained many of the ingredients of the film industry that was to follow: the actuality film (today we would call it a documentary) - workers leaving the Lumiere factory; drama - the train rushing into the station towards the camera; comedy - a little boy standing on a hosepipe followed by the bewildered gardener looking down the nozzle at the moment the boy takes his foot off the pipe; the trick film - demolishing a wall and then showing the film backwards so the wall appears to rebuild itself; and the best of home movies - Auguste and Mme Lumiere at home, with their small daughter in a high chair, being fed by father.

These films had been shown in France to photographic societies and the like during 1895. In England there were similar happenings. Birt Acres, the manager of a photographic plate firm, had devised, both in collaboration with Robert Paul and by himself, movie equipment with which he filmed the Derby in May, 1895. Here we have that other cinematic ingredient, the Topical, or as it became known, the newsreel.

Public shows, including the presentation of the French films in this country, spread during 1896. The first homes of moving pictures were the theatres and music halls. The film subjects included boxing matches, rough seas, trains coming into stations and out of tunnels, as well as a few fictional items, such as "The Arrest of a Pickpocket" and "The Soldier's Courtship". Most of these films were very short, lasting only about a minute or so. In the spring of 1896 Acres' camera was at work, probably with Acres himself operating it, at Yarmouth filming fishing boats leaving the harbour and children paddling on the beach. Acres usually included one of these Yarmouth films in his shows, together with the Royal films he had made and shown at Marlborough House before the Prince of Wales (later King Edward VII). The beach film was included in a programme at the Agricultural Hall in Norwich, now the home of Anglia Television, in January, 1897. It probably proved popular on that occasion as local scenes were always, and still are, of great interest to audiences. So must have been the "Prize Fight by Jem Mace and Burke", also in the programme, for Jem Mace was a Norwich man who took up boxing, in those days with bare fists, in the middle of the nineteenth century. He must have been about 65 when the

ONE OF MR. GILBERT'S
SURPRISE PROGRAMMES
COMMENCING TO-NIGHT, JAN. 11TH, 1897.
Something to Astonish the Amusement World at
Gilbert's Modern Circus
AGRICULTURAL HALL, NORWICH.

First Appearance of the
ROYAL
CINEMATOGRAPHE,
THE ANIMATED PHOTOGRAPHS,
Representing with Marvellous Accuracy Scenes of Everyday Life.
This is the first machine that was shown in England, and also the only one that has been before H.R.H. the
PRINCE OF WALES,
by special command. The Royal Films were taken direct at Marlborough House by the Prince's own request.
Selections will be made from the following :—
THE DERBY. BOXING KANGAROO.
THE SOUTH WESTERN RAILWAY AT DOVER.
A PRIZE FIGHT BY JEM MACE AND BURKE.
TOM MERRY, LIGHTNING CARICOONIST.
HIGHGATE TUNNEL: THE GOODS TRAIN.
YARMOUTH BEACH,
THE DANCING DOGS.
THE ROYAL FILMS.
1. Arrival of the Royal Party at Marlborough House.
2. Departure of the Royal Party from Marlborough House.
3. Garden Party on the Lawn at Marlborough House.
4. Arrival of the Prince and Suite.

Above: The Agricultural Hall, Norwich, is now the home of Anglia Television.

film was made, a remarkable age for an active pugilist. Mace was the landlord for a time of the Swan Tavern in Swan Lane, now the site of G.F.Butcher's drapery store. Often to be seen walking the streets of Norwich, he was even in old age a tall man with a splendid physique. It seems that he was still working in 1908, when seventy-seven, as a referee at a boxing match at a Norwich theatre. The films were obviously well received as they ran in Norwich for four weeks. Cecil Hepworth, an early film producer at this time travelling round the country with a cinematograph, had similar success at Halstead in Essex, where he was asked to repeat his programme of films fifteen times.

Queen Victoria's Diamond Jubilee Procession through London on June 22nd, 1897, was well covered by the early film makers, some with two and three cameras recording the occasion. The Jubilee films were shown all over the country, including Chelmsford Corn Exchange on October 1st and 2nd - over three months after the event.

Very few films from this period have survived. How interesting it would be to see members of the Photographic Convention parading before a camera as they came out of Yarmouth Town Hall in July, 1897, taken by Mr W.H. Prestwich, founder of a firm which has been described as one of the most important manufacturers of cinematographic equipment in Britain. Just after midday on 14th July, the film was rushed to London to be developed and printed. The completed film was back in Yarmouth in time for it to be shown in the Town Hall the following evening along with film of Queen Victoria's Diamond Jubilee procession taken earlier in the year. W.H. Prestwich was at the Yarmouth Photographic Convention with a trade exhibit staged by the Moto-Photo Supply Company, with which was also associated Mr J.A. Prestwich - possibly his son - a gifted engineer who not only gave his initials to the JAP motocycle but constructed some of the best cinematographic apparatus of those early years. "This is about one of the quickest bits of work we have heard of", said a report in the Photographic News of July 23rd, 1897, "and the Company are to be congratulated on having secured such a fine instrument which for projection is extremely steady and without any annoying flicker."

As the 19th century drew to a close, the cinematograph's popularity grew, mainly because it was seen at town and country fairs through the efforts of travelling showmen and lanternists.

Projector, operator and a set of films could be hired from Coe's of Norwich.

At that time, before cinemas and film renters, films were bought outright. The Warwick Trading Company had made a 125ft film of Norwich streets in 1902, the views being taken from the top of a tram travelling along Dereham Road, through Charing Cross, over Bank Plain and down Prince of Wales Road, and back by the Bell Hotel. The same year another film was made in the region, again in Yarmouth, showing sailing and steam drifters entering the harbour, followed by fish quay scenes. In one shot the herring, still on board the fishing boat, are seen being counted by hand, in what were known as long hundreds - a typical East Anglian method by which 130 fish or more equalled a hundred! The men counted in "warps" - that is four fish, two in each hand - a method which ceased to be used about 1908 when the quarter-cran basket was legalised as a measure. Next the fish girls are seen at work gutting the herring; a caption states that each girl does sixty-five a minute, but that is a bit optimistic, though perhaps the quickest girls did reach one a second.

In the early 1900s anyone could buy a cinematograph outfit for somewhere between ten and forty pounds, depending on whether it was for home use or for public shows. Coes in Norwich had a new projector ready for the winter season of 1902-03 which gave "a perfect picture, as steady as possible, brilliant, sharp, and distinct, and free from flicker". This was available for hire with an operator for entertainment shows, the customer selecting the programme from a list of sets of films available.

Carus Bedford, who dealt in photographic materials in Carr Street, Ipswich, bought a Bioscope projector and toured around Suffolk showing comedy, drama and trick films. "Cinematograph, Lantern and Limelight entertainments provided" ran his advertising material. His projector was rescued by Don Chipperfield in the late 1930s and is now on display in the East Anglian Film Archive, Bedford's films having been deposited in the National Film Archive.

Carus Bedford's 'Bioscope', a magic lantern cum cinematograph, beautifully restored for the Film Archive by Kim and Phil Archer.

Ronald Bates - Electrical engineer and film enthusiast.

The cameras of this period were large and cumbersome machines, made of mahogany and brass, and so heavy that they had to be used on a tripod. The more expensive versions held about 5½ minutes of film and had a focussing tube that enabled the operator to line up his shot by looking at the back of the stationary frame of film in the camera gate, a form of reflex viewing. The handle that operated the mechanism had to be turned at a constant speed of two revolutions per second; the operator whose excitement caused him to crank the handle too fast was no good at all - the film would be in slow motion when viewed. A camera of this type would have cost about £25.

Another Edwardian film enthusiast in East Anglia was Ronald Bates, an electrical engineer in Abbeygate Street, Bury St. Edmunds. When in July, 1907, two thousand performers took part in the "Bury St. Edmunds Great Historical Pageant", consisting of seven episodes in Bury history from the time of Boadicea to the founding of Edward VI's Grammar School in 1550, Ronald Bates recorded scenes from each episode. With those shots he produced a film running for twenty-five minutes, which was distributed by the Gaumont Company. According to Clifford Manning of Ely, who has done much research into early film shows, Ronald Bates' film was shown on September 7th at Newmarket Town Hall. The show ended in tragedy however, for just before the interval a film caught fire, the audience panicked, and three lives were lost.

A scene from Ronald Bates' 1907 film of the Bury St. Edmunds pageant.

A typical camera of the Edwardian period. This is a Moy & Bastie hand-turned machine. The handle had to be turned at two revolutions per second.

Charles Aldous, a photographer in White Lion Street, Norwich, also had a cine camera, with which he recorded scenes of Horning Regatta in 1908. He set his camera up on the bank near the Swan Inn and filmed anything interesting that happened, including an interlude when the pleasure steamer Queen of the Broads ploughed triumphantly through the proceedings, fully laden with Broads sightseers. At the end of the film Mr. Aldous recorded the prize giving, with the Edwardians in their best clothes.

Right: Charles Aldous the sporting photographer.
Below: Horning Regatta, 1908.

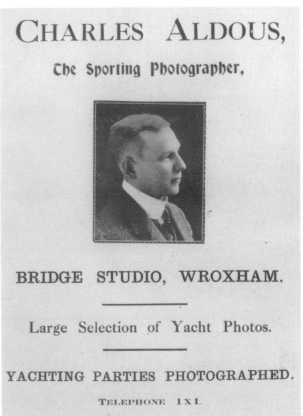

CHARLES ALDOUS,

The Sporting Photographer,

BRIDGE STUDIO, WROXHAM.

Large Selection of Yacht Photos.

YACHTING PARTIES PHOTOGRAPHED.

TELEPHONE 1 X 1.

On October 25th, 1909, King Edward VII visited Norwich "to review and to present guidons and colours to certain units of the Territorial Forces in Norfolk, and to lay the foundation stone of the extensions to the Norfolk and Norwich Hospital", as the official programme put it. A cameraman from A.E. Coe and Son, photographers and opticians of 32, London Street, Norwich, covered the occasion, and the film was shown the next day at the Thatched Assembly Rooms which stood next to Bonds Store on All Saints Green. Like so many films of the era Coe's film of the visit has suffered from decomposition over the years and only about ten minutes of the original print survive. Records show that other films were made of a Christmas cattle show in Norwich and a Territorial Army parade at Ipswich. In 1912 Southwold Town Council agreed that a film should be made of the town, and some films were made of Lowestoft in 1913. In the 1912 catalogue of Kinemacolor, an early colour system, there were "The Yarmouth Herring Industry" and "The Glories of the Norfolk Broads." Clifford Manning's researches show that a number of local films were made in the Cambridge area, including the opening of the Midsummer Fair in 1912, Cottenham Races in 1913 and a nine minute speeded-up film of the building of the Playhouse Cinema. It is a great pity that these and other early films of East Anglian life were not preserved.

THATCHED ASSEMBLY ROOMS,

NORWICH.

TUESDAY, OCTOBER 26th, 1909, at 7 p.m. and 9 p.m., and
WEDNESDAY, OCTOBER 27th, 1909, at 4 p.m., 7 p.m., and 9 p.m.

A. E. COE & SON

WILL EXHIBIT

Cinematograph Views

**Taken specially by them from the best positions
(having obtained sole rights), of the**

King's Visit to Norwich

INCLUDING

Laying the Foundation Stone at the Hospital,
The Review on Mousehold,
Inspection of the Veterans, etc., etc.,

also, by arrangement with the Gaumont Co., Ltd., the **Extraordinary and Unique**
Films of

Shackleton's Dash to the Pole

As taken by him on his wonderful journey.

These Films were Exhibited at Balmoral by Special Command of His
Majesty the King.

Selections by an efficient Orchestra under the leadership of Mr. Walter Gemmer.

Reserved Seats (numbered), 2/-; Second Seats, 1/-; and a limited number, 6d.
Children Half-Price to Matinée only.

Plan of Hall at

A. E. COE & SON, 32, London Street, Norwich.

Coe's poster for the film of the King's visit.

Right: King Edward VII arriving at the Drill Hall in Chapel Field Road, Norwich during his visit in 1909.

Newsreels
(The Animated Newspaper)

As the film industry became established, so cinemas appeared. In April, 1909, the Gem at Great Yarmouth was described as "one of the handsomest halls devoted to motion pictures in Great Britain. During the summer season a continuous show is given and as many as ten thousand people have paid in one day", said The Bioscope, a trade magazine of the time. The Gem was "under the personal direction of Mr Charles B.Cochrane", and "besides the movie projector a powerful Russian lantern is used for illustrated songs, topical slides and announcements."

A month earlier, the programme at the The Gem consisted of "Tragic Love", "Visit to a Cattle Ranch", "The Bohemian Girl" and twenty topical news slides. Walter Tyler, of Waterloo Road, London, supplied weekly topical slide sets. The April 17th, 1909, issue consisted of "How they do things in Vienna", "The London Child's Holiday", "London's new Underground Reservoir", "The Monaco Motorboat races", and "The crisis at Constantinople".

Slides flashed on the screen for advertising announcements and for local news items have always been used in cinemas, to recent times. In 1959 the result of the F.A.Cup semi-final between Norwich City and Luton was scratched on a slide and shown on the Norvic cinema screen as soon as news came through. But topical slides are really a relic of magic lantern days, and the film industry soon found a new way of presenting everyday happenings with the "Animated Newspaper" or newsreels as they were called later.

One of the first was the Warwick Bioscope Chronicle, joined in 1910 by two other newsreels, Pathe's Animated Gazette and Gaumont Graphic. The latter, at first produced weekly with two hundred copies being sent out, soon moved to twice-weekly issues. Royal events were regular ingredients of these newsreels and in 1911, when the Royal Show was held at Crown Point, Norwich, a Pathe cameraman was there to record the King's visit to the Show. A year later King George V was back to watch army manoeuvres in West Suffolk.

Newsreels of this time were quite varied in content and international in outlook. The contents of a Pathe Gazette issued in the last week of June, 1912, consisted of shots of two planes that had

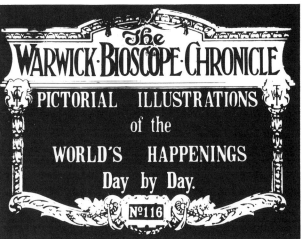

collided in a French military aviation disaster, students' revels in London, with shots of art students in the Botanical Gardens, the Battle of Flowers in Paris and, near Chelmsford, Essex, the marriage of pioneer airman Claude Grahame-White and Miss Dorothy Chadwell Taylor. In London there is a sequence of the coaching marathon and at Windsor the Prince of Wales and the King reviewed members of the St. John Ambulance Brigade. The reason the wedding of Grahame-White was part of a national newsreel was that not only was he a famous aviator of the time but he arrived at the wedding in his own aeroplane. This item would have been seen all over the country, but not all stories were. Audiences outside East Anglia would not have been interested in Pathe's four-minute record of a swimming race down the River Gipping at Ipswich, for the Bulstrode Cup, in 1913.

By this time the newsreel companies had divided the country into districts - principally so that events could be covered by an area cameraman. Local stories would occasionally be filmed and joined to the main newsreel.

There was plenty of hard news about in the First World War newsreels, but very rarely did the news have anything to do with East Anglia. An exception was the surrender of the German U-boat fleet in 1918 when some 150 submarines, met by the Harwich Force commanded by Admiral Sir Reginald Tyrwhitt off Harwich, made their way into the River Stour, where they were moored. The Gaumont Newsreel of the surrender, "Admiral Tyrwhitt's cruiser squadron takes over the German pirate craft", shows an airship, possibly R23, over one of the warships, shots of various U-boats passing the camera, and finally British sailors looking after the German crews. "Q Ships", a British feature film made in 1928 about the work of armed and disguised merchant ships used in the war to combat U-boats, has a short sequence at the end of newsreel shots of the submarines at anchor in the Stour.

Chelmsford.
FAMOUS AVIATOR MARRIED.
Mr. Grahame White and Miss Dorothy Chadwell Taylor.
Bride-groom and guests fly to the Wedding.

PATHE FRÈRES CINEMA L?

Frame two: Claude Graham-White flying to his wedding.

Frame three: Claude Graham-White and his new wife leaving Widford Church after their wedding.

Regular events which were not really news at all were often covered. The well-known goings on in the Pyefleet Channel off Brightlingsea at the opening of the Colchester oyster fishery season were, and still are, covered by the news cameras. Only a few years ago local television filmed this colourful annual event in September when the Mayor of Colchester and members of the Corporation, accompanied by members of the Colne Fishery Board, partake of gin and gingerbread and toast the Monarch aboard an oyster smack. The ceremony continues with the bewigged Town Clerk reading the traditional proclamation and the Mayor hauling aboard the first dredge of the season. The last shot is normally of a slightly reluctant Mayor trying to swallow an oyster.

In the 1920s there were several newsreel companies issuing twice-weekly editions, and there was great rivalry between them. In the trade they had facetious names for each other. Pathe Gazette was known as Pathetic Gazette; Gaumont Graphic was Gruesome Graphic; Empire Screen News was Impure Screen News and Topical Budget was Comical Budget. Some of the companies also produced interest shorts known as cine-magazines which we will hear more about later.

Four frames showing the opening of the oyster season in Pyefleet creek in 1920.

Above: The R33 at Pulham, ten days before a gale damaged her and blew her across the North Sea.

What sort of stories did the newsreel companies film in East Anglia and how did they fit in with the national issues of the day? The answer to the last part is that they didn't. It was only Royalty, nationally known personalities visiting East Anglia or disasters that brought the region into focus for the rest of the country. Admittedly there was in the 1920s a great interest in aviation matters and when the airship R33 was operating from Pulham in April 1925 a short sequence was taken there, but otherwise the newsreels filmed only innocuous and often frivolous local stories. In 1927 Topical Budget covered the amateur skating championships at Lingay Fen, near Cambridge, won by C.W.Horn, a champion cyclist and skater of the time. At Norwich Pathe filmed the Air Pageant at Mousehold Aerodrome, arranged to promote the Norfolk and Norwich Aeroplane Club on February 25th, 1927. A variety of aeroplanes visited Mousehold that day and the Lord Mayor, Charles Robert Bignold, put on his flying gear, complete with his chain of office on top, and took to the air. Later in the year, on Sunday, October 9th, Private B.A.Withers, a Norwich ex-serviceman who had lost a leg at the Battle of Gaza, unveiled the Norwich War Memorial at the east end of the Guildhall, the site chosen by Sir Edwin Lutyens. When the City Hall was built in 1938, the Memorial was moved to a Garden of Remembrance at the back of the Market Place.

Below: C. W. Horn, champion skater.

Above: The Lord Mayor of Norwich, Charles Bignold, preparing for his flight from Mousehold airfield in 1927.

The newsreels and the cine-magazines often looked at East Anglia for its picturesque scenes and curious ways. In 1927 Topical Budget filmed Mr Chesney selling water at Docking. At that time, when water was scarce in this part of high Norfolk and the main supply came from a well 237 feet deep, Mr Chesney pumped up water into his water cart and then went round Docking selling it for a halfpenny a pail. This was used mainly for drinking and cooking purposes, soft water from the rainwater tub being used for washing. A year after the film was made the price was increased to 1d a pail, a lot of money then, but the following year, 1929, a water tower was built and a few taps appeared around Docking for people to collect water whenever they wished.

The film of Mr Chesney delivering water is short, consisting of nine shots. Then there follows a sort of joke by the London cameraman, for a caption states "Where there's a will there's a way" and we see a car standing axle deep in the village pond being scrubbed by its driver. The film is a fascinating glimpse of life in rural East Anglia. So in a way is "A Railway that is a real joke", a short film of the narrow gauge Southwold railway in its last days of working in the Gaumont Mirror series. This cine magazine which ran for a while in the late 1920s contained stories and scenes which did not get into the Gaumont Graphic newsreel, as well as specially shot material.

The railway, running between Halesworth and Southwold, was opened on Wednesday, 24th September, 1879, and closed fifty years later. 3 feet in gauge, the line had distinctive engines and

rolling stock. Many humorous stories grew up round the railway, many of them true; the train did sometimes wait for regular passengers if they overslept, and it was a fact that the engine driver faced imprisonment if he exceeded 16 miles per hour. The closure of a railway line was uncommon at the time and, coupled with the eccentricity of the Southwold Railway, was sufficiently newsworthy for the Gaumont Mirror to record it all - complete with comical captions.

Southwold Railway scenes during the last week of operation in April, 1929.

The film shows the railway's four engines, two in working order, Wenhaston and Blyth, and two laid up at the depot, Halesworth and Southwold, as they were named. The film's key sequences show a mixed train leaving Southwold station, a rural view of the line with the train chugging through the shot, an interior view of a crowded carriage with a ticket collector at work, and a slightly comic shot of a signalman pulling down a signal as the train approaches. At Halesworth, we see one of the goods wagons being unloaded. The London caption writers spelt Halesworth "Hailsworth" and one caption states "It has been known to complete the journey of nine miles in fifty minutes." No wonder the new-fangled motor buses took away the railway's trade. One 35mm copy of this film in the Archive ends with a sequence of the last run on April 11th, 1929, probably filmed by Mr.James Blyth of the Southwold Cinema and joined on the end of the Gaumont Mirror film which he subsequently obtained.

Two other stories from the "Gaumont Mirror" about Southwold show fishermen mending their nets in a picturesque sequence filmed on the beach, and a film of a private zoo in the town run by Mr Hill, an undertaker and cabinet-maker. "Strange pets and their tricks" shows rabbits and parrots pulling model carriages, and white mice on a replica roundabout. According to local legend Mr Hill provided the cockerel for Pathe title sequences.

"Eve's Film Review" (1921-1933) was a silent cine magazine aimed at women. Some East Anglian items that have survived from this show the Broads in the late 1920s as well as some surprising sections, such as the new electrically operated swing bridge near Beccles in 1925.

The unusual was sought after by the producers of these cine magazines, an example being a short sequence in a "Pathe Pictorial" of 1939 showing a Yarmouth fisherman making a lady's hat out of bits of rope. The recording of stage, film and radio artists doing their "party piece" was a regular ingredient, and these are sought after today as they are often the only surviving record of music hall stars and celebrities. One Essex novelty dance duo Carr and Parr were filmed by Pathe in 1927 showing three of their routines. Two of these were to the popular music "The doll dance" and "Tea for two" but the silent film audience probably never knew that. Carr and Parr had appeared at the 1926 Royal Command Performance at the Alhambra in London.

The lavender harvest at Hunstanton was one of the subjects of a pictorial in 1948, and in the early 1950s the Birds Eye factory at Yarmouth was shown with the latest method of quick freezing peas. These industrial processes are of interest as methods have changed or the business has ceased. The weaving mill at Halstead has now gone, but there is a sequence in an "Ace Cine Magazine" which shows synthetic material being made in the mid-1930s.

The Children's Film Foundation's "Our Magazine" appeared periodically, and this occasionally contained regional stories. Number 15 has a good sequence of artist Harry Pettit and his two daughters who lived in a water-mill in Ardleigh in Essex. The girls lead a country life, riding through the lanes on horses, canoeing on the mill pond and collecting grasses and leaves for their father's work.

The cine magazines which ran between eight and ten minutes disappeared from the cinema screens in the 1960s. In 1959 when Gaumont British News ceased operating, the "Look at Life" films were produced but with a limited life of ten years. A more specialised series consisted of the magazine films produced by Pathe for the R.A.F. called "Astra Gazettes", for showing in camp cinemas. They were still going in 1968 when they filmed a story about Mrs Ada Roe who was running her dairy shop at Lowestoft at the age of 110. The film goes on to show a woman pilot bringing in a Lightning aircraft to Coltishall where she receives a certificate as a member of the "1,000 miles per hour club".

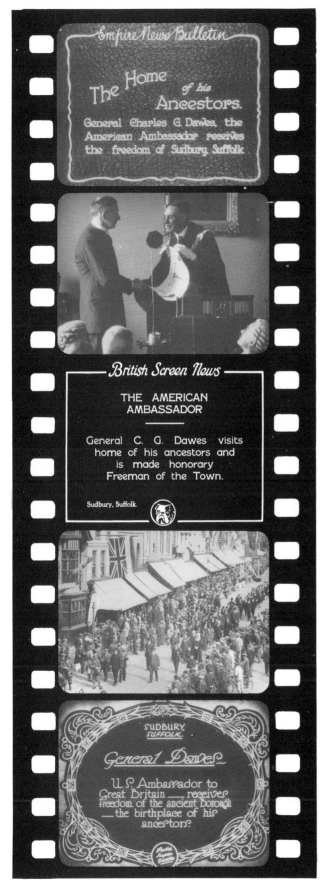

In 1929, a local event on October 1st in Sudbury was put out by four national newsreel companies. The American Ambassador of the time, General Charles Gates Dawes, found that his ancestors had come from the Suffolk town, a stonemason named William Dawes having sailed in the "Planter" to New England in 1635. Topical Budget, British Screen News, Empire News Bulletin and Pathe Super Gazette all covered the story of General Dawes receiving the Freedom of the Borough of Sudbury, with shots of the Mayor, Edmund Fitzgerald, handing over the document in the Town Hall, followed by scenes in the Market Place.

Also in 1929 Movietone imported from America the first sound equipment for newsreels, and on June 9th their first issue appeared with a sub-title "It speaks for Itself".The very earliest example of sound recording of an East Anglian item so far found contains no commentary, only the actual sound recorded as the camera filmed a procession of clergy entering the West Door of Norwich Cathedral on August 13th, 1930, for the 1300th anniversary of the founding of the Diocese of East Anglia. The Eastern Evening News reported that "the crowd watched with interest the taking of a talking motion picture" but in fact there was no talking, only the hubbub of footsteps and distant conversations.

On October 21st, 1930, when the Haven Bridge at Yarmouth was opened by the Prince of Wales (later Duke of Windsor), Pathe not only recorded the natural sounds but also the Prince of Wales's short speech. The quality of this is not good by

modern standards, as the microphone was too far away from His Royal Highness, but his words can just be heard. Both he and his brother, the Duke of York, later King George VI, were nervous speakers. At Yarmouth the Prince is seen speaking too quickly and unable to keep still; and in film of the opening of Norwich City Hall in 1938 his brother, then the King, had difficulty in getting words out.

The rest of the Yarmouth film shows the Prince of Wales inspecting the fishing boats and touring the "Great Yards" where the fisher girls were at work gutting the herring. This must be the first recording ever made of the girls singing as they worked. A little commentary is sprinkled over this sequence; by the sound of it this commentary was done live at Yarmouth rather than recorded after at the studios, as was normal practice later. This represents no more than a primitive attempt at sound, but the evocative recording of the cheering crowds and the triumphant blasts from the fishing boats' whistles overcomes the inadequacies of the

Below: The Prince of Wales speaking at the opening of the Haven Bridge in Yarmouth in 1930. Note the microphones in the left-hand corner.

system. At this time silent and sound newsreels were running side by side, and in fact the Haven Bridge opening and the Norwich Cathedral celebrations were also filmed in silent versions by other companies.

In the 1930s the main newsreels were Universal Talking News, formerly Empire News Bulletin, British Movietone News, Gaumont British News, Pathe Super Sound Gazette and British Paramount News. They continued on into the 1950s with some title changes. In October 1934, Pathe covered the Mildenhall to Melbourne air race, the preparations and the take-off at dawn on October 20th being filmed. This great race was won by C.W.Scott and Campbell Black flying a de Havilland Comet named "Grosvenor House" which covered the 11,300 miles in 71 hours.

Above: King George VI meeting players at Norwich Football Ground during his visit to open the City Hall in 1938.

It was while in Mildenhall that the cameraman spotted coal being delivered by Ivy Base. The sight of a woman coal merchant was obviously unusual, so the cameraman filmed her at work, thus catching a story on the spot of rural ways in Suffolk - just like Mr.Chesney selling water around Docking in 1927.

A regular Suffolk subject was the annual Duke of York's camp held on Southwold Common each August which brought together boys from all walks of life. In one film the Duke is shown operating the camera, and the actual shots he took are in the newsreel. Also filmed was his visit, as King George VI, to Norwich in 1938 for the opening of the new City Hall. After the opening the King went to Carrow Road football ground to watch Norwich City play Millwall, while Queen Elizabeth opened a new maternity wing at the Norfolk and Norwich Hospital, built as a memorial to Captain Geoffrey Colman.

Two extracts showing men of the Auxiliary Fire Service on exercise at Littleport, Cambridgeshire.

The outbreak of war in 1939 took the attention of the newsreel cameramen away from East Anglia, but on Saturday 8th March, 1941, Movietone made a special short film at Littleport in the Cambridgeshire Fens to help raise £30,000 for the town's War Weapons Week. The money, working out at £6 per inhabitant, was for the purchase of weapons for British soldiers. The film shows the people of Littleport and the men of the Auxiliary Fire Service exercising to stirring background music. The film was shown a few days later at Littleport's Regal Cinema, where it fortunately survived until found by the Archive a few years ago, and so can still be viewed.

East Anglia was never really on the newsreel cameraman's beat. Bad storms near Mildenhall in 1947 brought Paramount News along to see the damage to the crops; the 1953 floods which brought such a trail of destruction to the East Coast provided a story for all the newsreels; and a

new course for the Cambridgeshire at Newmarket in 1951 was covered by Universal News. Incidentally, it is worth recording that in the 1950s Gaumont British News would make an individual title for a particular cinema consisting of ''The . . . Cinema presents Gaumont British News''. The title would be retained by the cinema and joined on to the new issue when it arrived. Gaumont British News ceased operations in 1959, no doubt affected by the arrival of a second television news service.

Most of the other newsreels had gone by February, 1970, when Pathe News ceased production. The last East Anglian story in this newsreel was probably the report of the Old People's Day Centre in the redundant railway station buildings at Reedham in 1969. Movietone survived the longest, carrying on until May, 1979, ending not only fifty years of their own production but one of the cinema's most engaging ingredients.

A poster in a shop window advertising that British Movietone News will be making a film in Littleport as part of the town's war weapons week on Saturday March 8th 1941. The film was shown on March 10th at the Regal Cinema. No doubt Albert Wright, saddler by profession and local and district councillor contributed his £6 towards Littleport's campaign.

Local Newsreels – see yourself on the big screen

"Three Cheers for the Vaudeville" said a film made in 1914 of the children's matinee audience outside the Colchester cinema of that name, later known as the Empire. It stood in Mersea Road close to where the St. Botolph's roundabout is now.

The cinema, Colchester's first, was three years old when the owner, David Ager, asked his son to make a five-minute film showing the large crowd of youngsters who went to the matinee on October 3rd. As many as possible of the children outside the cinema were filmed, the simple idea being that they would come again whenever the film was shown, hopefully accompanied by their parents. A full cinema was a happy sight for the owner.

Scenes of local interest had been used in cinema programmes as an extra draw for many years, but there was a difference between hiring ready-made film of familiar scenes and having a film made especially for your cinema. There were companies ready to come and film local stories for enterprising cinema managements. "Local Film Subjects our Speciality ... Experienced Photographers sent to any part of the country" ran an advertisement for the London Cinematograph Company in 1909. But the heyday of the local newsreel was undoubtedly the Twenties and Thirties.

The main purveyor in Suffolk of these occasional local items was the Bostock cinema circuit, which grew out of E.H.Bostock's theatre and cinema interests before the First World War. E.H.Bostock was responsible for the Ipswich Hippodrome which was opened on March 27th, 1905, and had a varied career as a theatre, cinema and bingo hall, finally being demolished in 1985. These ventures were not confined to East Anglia, E.H.Bostock having a cinema near Glasgow in 1909. At that time, however, he was better known for his Bostock and Wombwell travelling menagerie, part of which travelled to America to appear in the movies in 1923. Bostock's son Douglas built up the East Anglian cinema circuit by acquiring and building cinemas from Rayleigh in Essex to Wells in Norfolk and as far west as St.Ives in Huntingdonshire, or Cambridgeshire as it is now. Douglas bought a 35mm movie camera which was used by Harry West, who spent all his working life with Bostock's, from projectionist to cinema manager, to film many local events. More than twenty of

A typical early cinema. This is Poole's Picture Palace in Tower Street, Ipswich opened in 1909.

these short items have survived, due to the foresight of Terry Neeves of Ipswich and Michael Cutting of Great Blakenham.

The majority of these surviving "Bostock Gazettes", as they were known, are of Ipswich, and through them it is possible to see what was happening in the town in the late twenties. Sequences show crowds watching the 1st Battalion of the Suffolk Regiment parading on the Cornhill during a recruiting march through the county, a Conservative Fete at the Chantry, and Prince Henry (later the Duke of Gloucester) visiting Ipswich to open the Gainsborough bicentenary exhibition. Gainsborough was born at Sudbury in 1727, and there were festivities and a ceremony in his birthplace

Children outside the Vaudeville Cinema in Colchester on October 3rd, 1914.

BOSTOCK GAZETTE.

BRITISH LEGION FETE.

Wednesday, July 3rd, 1929.

Above: A helpful frame from the sequence from which the picture below is taken.

Above: Decorated motor cars on the A12 taking "poor" children on an outing to Little Glemham on July 12th, 1930.

as well as in Ipswich in 1927. A local newsreel was made of the Sudbury events, but it is not known by whom. A "Bostock Gazette" was made in 1928 of the opening of Ipswich Golf Club on June 16th with Henry Cotton immaculately dressed in plus fours and natty shoes. But there was a bit of hard news as well when Wrinch's furniture factory in Portman Road was destroyed by fire. The fire put 300 men out of work and damaged the Labour Exchange close by, which must have posed a bit of a problem. This story may possibly have been filmed or edited by someone other than Harry West as the titles are of an unusual form. Other films made around this time show Armistice Day at Ipswich, a poor children's outing to Glemham, a visit of the Prince of Wales to Ipswich and the Ipswich and District Motor-cycle Club speed trials at Shrubland Park, Barham, where the motorbikes and cars speed up the drive amidst clouds of dust.

Below: Part of the British Legion fete parade in Christchurch Park, Ipswich.

There is also a record of the Suffolk Show in Christchurch Park, Ipswich, during the first week of June, 1927, but it appears that this was filmed not by Harry West but by a contract cameraman from London, John Hutchins. He worked for various newsreel companies during his professional life and was at that time employed by Topical Budget. Perhaps it was the success of this film that led Douglas Bostock to buy a camera.

Harry West's films were simple recordings lasting only a few minutes, part of the footage being made up of crowd scenes. Shots of the crowds were essential to get people into the cinema to see themselves on the big screen, either at the Lyceum or the Hippodrome in Ipswich. As soon as the film was shot it was sent to Gaumont in London for processing and for a print to be made. In those days before colour film was in common use many films were tinted; that is, the scene or shot was

Below: Motor cycle speed trials held at Shrubland Park drive. This event was put on by the Ipswich and District Motor Cycle Club in aid of the Ipswich and East Suffolk Hospital.

Above: Prince Henry in Ipswich to open the Gainsborough Exhibition on October 7th, 1927.

Above: The Suffolk Show of 1927 was held in Christchurch Park, Ipswich on June 2nd and 3rd.

coloured blue or green, depending on the mood required. A local screen advertisement for the building of Witham Cinema was tinted purple throughout. Harry West ordered his prints to be either in black-and-white or light amber, the latter being very popular and pleasing on the eye. In the Wrinch film the night-time shots of flames are tinted red. The "Bostock Gazettes" do not seem to have been edited at all but were shown as shot; a sequence of the Easter Air Display at the old Hadleigh airfield on April 9th, 1928, even includes a short shot of the ground taken when the camera was accidentally switched on as Harry West was walking along.

Usually a title was prepared and joined on to the front. Sometimes this read "Bostock Gazette" and was followed by a caption naming the event or occasion, then the date, but this was not always the case; quite often there was no title at all,

Below: The Hippodrome in Ipswich was opened on March 27th, 1905. Around 1928 it appeared in one of Harry West's local newsreels, but the occasion is unknown.

making identification and dating very difficult - there are some stories from the Bostock collection in the Archive of which nothing is known.

Other local newsreels for Clacton, Colchester, Wisbech, Yarmouth and Norwich exist in the Archive , the Norwich items including a carnival and the opening of Eaton Park by the Prince of Wales. George Swain, the Norwich photographer who had a shop in St. Giles, was friendly with a cinema manager in the city and with his son, also George and also a photographer, recorded some local events on cine film. Perhaps the most important was the funeral in 1919 of Edith Cavell, whose execution by the Germans in 1915 had aroused great public feeling throughout Britain. When her body was brought back to Norwich on May 15th, 1919, it is said people lined the railway track from London to Norwich in silent tribute. The daughter of the Vicar of Swardeston, she had

Below: The Lyceum Theatre in Carr Street, Ipswich, was acquired by Bostocks in 1920, but closed in 1936.

Many films have been made of the annual Co-op Day in Colchester, and the earliest - made about 1925 - was printed on safety film (non-flam) and was tinted light amber. These instructions were scratched on the leader of the film with the name of the company printing the film - Gaumont. Safety film was used when films were shown in local halls and for private shows.

taken up nursing and was matron of a Belgian hospital when that country was overrun by the German armies in 1914. Knowing the possible consequences she helped conceal British and allied officers and enabled them to escape from occupied territory. She was arrested, tried by court martial and shot on October 12th, 1915. The film of her funeral in Norwich shows the coffin being removed from the gun carriage on which it had been conveyed from Thorpe Station and carried by soldiers, one of whom had been helped to freedom by Edith Cavell, through crowds to Life's Green, beside the east end of Norwich Cathedral. The annual memorial service that was held around her grave for many years appears in some later films in the Archive.

Local newsreels were made in the 1920s in and around Cambridge and shown at the "Kinema" and "Victoria" cinemas. They were made by Eric Pointer of A.J.Pointer and Sons, the proprietors of these cinemas. One film showed the Cambridgeshire Hunt meeting on Market Hill on Boxing Day, 1925. Do any of these Cambridge films still survive in a cellar or attic somewhere?

Southwold was also known for its local newsreels. These film reports were the equivalent of stories in today's television programmes "About Anglia" or "Look East". They were not only shown as soon as possible after the event but also on 'high days and holidays' at the Southwold Cinema, opened in 1912 in the Assembly Rooms in York Road. In 1921 the cinema was bought by the Crick family and Mrs Crick's son by a former marriage, James Blyth, became manager. James Blyth acquired a hand-turned movie camera and began recording events in Southwold for showing in his cinema.

On October 31st, 1926, Henry Smith, mate of a Lowestoft drifter, jumped overboard fully clothed to rescue a colleague from drowning, and for his heroism Smith was awarded the Stanhope Gold Medal for the bravest deed of the year and was made an honorary freeman of the Borough of Southwold. On April 28th, 1927, a large crowd gathered to watch the Mayor present Henry Smith with the medal and the scroll recording his admission to the freedom, the ceremony being filmed by James Blyth.

The highlight of the year at Southwold was, and still is to some extent, Trinity Fair, opened at noon on Trinity Monday when the Town Clerk read an ancient proclamation. As there is only one way into Southwold, the showmen trundled up the High Street at all hours of the Sunday, upsetting some of the inhabitants. It was agreed therefore that the fair people would assemble outside the town and come into Southwold in one long cavalcade on the Sunday evening. For the 1928 fair Mr Blyth set up his camera on the flat roof which then existed at the King's Head and turned his camera as the procession rolled by, the film

Above: Edith Cavell's cortege arriving at Norwich Cathedral.
Below: A paddle steamer leaving Clacton Pier about 1930, part of a local newsreel.

Above: Henry Smith receiving the Stanhope Gold Medal for his bravery in rescuing a colleague from drowning.

Above: Southwold Cinema in York Road, with a publicity float in 1927.

Below: Trinity Fair arriving at Southwold in 1928.

showing showmens' waggons pulled by horses and traction engines. He even turned the camera handle very slowly at one point so that the procession appeared to have speeded up - always good for a laugh. Next he filmed the reading by the Town Clerk of the charter which has allowed Southwold to hold a fair since the time of Henry VII. The next bit of the ritual, the Mayor having the first ride on the roundabout, was at that time relatively new, having been introduced in 1922 when the then Mayor, Mr. A.J. Critten, accompanied by his officials, jumped on the roundabout to claim a ride. Their bit of fun caught on and the practice still continues today.

Mr. Blyth might well have recorded every Trinity Fair for a number of years, but unfortunately very little of his work survives, piles of rotting film having to be thrown away around 1960. Two other stories of Southwold life worth mentioning show a paddle tug towing away the old Southwold to Walberswick ferry and a new one named "Blyth" taking over, and the wreck of the Lowestoft smack "Evela" which came ashore in thick fog on January 9th, 1934. The crew were taken off by the Southwold lifeboat "Mary Scott". Mr Blyth's film shows the "Evela" on the beach, from which she was eventually refloated and, after repair, put back into service.

James Blyth retired in 1959 after 38 years as manager of the Southwold Cinema. The cinema closed only two years later. For some time it was used as a repository by Blyth Removals before being demolished in 1983. James Blyth's few remaining films were kept by a local historian, Mr. Barrett Jenkins, another Southwold film maker, of whom we shall hear more later.

Above: James Blyth, manager of the Southwold Cinema and film-maker.

The Commercial World

In 1920, Valentia Steer, the first editor of Pathe's Animated Gazette, wrote "It is estimated on reliable authority that more than thirty million people in Great Britain go to the pictures every week" and that "the cinematograph is now classed as the fifth biggest industry in the world". The film makers were in it to make money, and so were the cinema owners. An unknown author, on the side of the customer, wrote later "We do not go to be instructed: we go to be entertained. Sitting in the dark in a comfortable seat, we can forget the worry and boredom of our own life, and live in that richer and more exciting world upon the screen. If the men are handsomer, the women more beautiful and virtue more rapidly rewarded than in real life, so much the better. That amongst other things is what we pay for - to have our fantasies fulfilled, our day-dreaming done for us".

Fictional films are outside the scope of this book, but it is worth remembering a few of the feature and second feature films shot either whole or in part in East Anglia. In the silent film days there was "The Rolling Road", a desert island story with Carlyle Blackwell filmed at Yarmouth in 1927; "The House of Marney", a melodrama set on the Essex coast, made in 1927 with Alma Taylor and John Longden, and a film made at Salhouse on the Norfolk Broads with Guy Newall and Ivy Duke, a pin-up girl of the time, in which the wherry "Forget me not" played a prominent part.

It is difficult to imagine Ipswich as a sort of British Walt Disney centre, but this is what Roland Davies, a young local artist, envisaged when he set up Roland Davies Cartoon Co. Ltd., an animation studio in Museum Street, Ipswich, in the mid 1930s. At its peak forty-three people, many from Ipswich Art School, worked in the studios on a series of cartoons featuring Steve the Horse - a character created by Roland Davies that appeared in a strip cartoon called "Come on Steve" in the Sunday Express. The films were very similar in gags and animation to the American output of the time. Carl Giles, the well-known cartoonist trained the animators and tracers who worked on the six

Manningtree Cinema about 1925.

Above: Steve the Horse.

Steve films - "Cinderella Steve", "Steve in Bohemia", "Steve of the River", "Steve steps out", "Steve's treasure-hunt" and "Steve's cannon crackers". Giles had been trained in Wardour Street as an animator since he left school at fourteen. He worked on the first cartoon in technicolor in Britain for Alexander Korda, and when his contract ended was invited to join the Disney team in Hollywood, but for domestic reasons, declined the offer and joined Roland Davies at Ipswich. A seventh "Steve" cartoon was to have been filmed in colour, but it never got beyond the planning stage because the studio folded up.

Below: When a trailer was not available sometimes slides were used to advertise a forthcoming film. Sticky tape blotted out the edge announcements which were not appropriate.

In 1939 about nineteen million people a week went to the cinema, and in wartime this rose to thirty million. During the Second World War every programme had to include a government propaganda film of some sort. Harry Watt's "Target for Tonight", a feature documentary made partly at Mildenhall in 1941, is said to have been seen by fifty million people. In the same year Eric Portman, Googie Withers and Bernard Miles, amongst others, starred in the Michael Powell - Emeric Pressburger film "One of Our Aircraft is Missing", which contained sequences shot at King's Lynn. Two years later the same team of film makers, again with Googie Withers but also joined by Ralph Richardson, were back at Lynn for "The Silver Fleet", a story of U-boats and the Dutch Resistance.

In 1944 Peter Hawkins, then a projectionist at the Majestic Cinema in Lynn, was asked by John Boulting to run the rushes of a semi-documentary being made at RAF Marham, "Journey Together", starring Richard Attenborough and Edward G. Robinson. Peter Hawkins received five shillings for showing the previous day's takes after the last cinema show.

In the 1940s film crews twice visited Blickling Hall in Norfolk, first in 1945 for "The Wicked Lady", with Margaret Lockwood and James Mason, and again two years later to film the technicolor period feature "Jassy" with Dennis Price, Patricia Roc and Margaret Lockwood. In 1947 Flixton Hall near Bungay was used in a children's adventure story "The Secret Tunnel", and a yachting film "Ha'penny Breeze", was made at Pin Mill a few years later.

"Conflict of Wings" with John Gregson, a story of an East Anglian community fighting to save a bird sanctuary, was filmed in 1953 around Hickling, and the River Orwell was in 1954 the backdrop for "The Sea Shall Not Have Them", a nail-biting story about a ditched aircraft's crew adrift in an inflatable dinghy, starring Dirk Bogarde and Michael Redgrave. The Orwell was again used for sequences in "Yangtse Incident", a 1957 film about the British frigate H.M.S. Amethyst trapped in the Yangtse River by Communist Chinese batteries. Richard Todd and William Hartnell starred.

Perhaps the best known of the East Anglian made feature films up to this time was "Barnacle Bill", one of the last of the Ealing comedies, made in 1957. It starred Alec Guinness as the captain of a pier - that at Hunstanton.

Then, as now, the cinema programmes included advertisements, both local and national. In the country cinemas local advertising, from outfitters

Above: A frame from a roll of advertisements shown at the Haymarket in Norwich in 1930.

and ironmongers to the local chimney sweep, was more likely to be on slides than on film. A roll of advertisements shown in 1930 at the Haymarket Cinema in Norwich included Henry Jarvis and Sons, Complete House Furnishers - known as the "Slumber Specialists" - of St. Benedict's Street; Batterbee and Son, tailors, hatters and hosiers, of 43 Magdalen Street; G.S. Jarrett, furniture remover and owner of saloon cars for weddings, of 62 Devonshire Street; Sissen and Bugdale, builders of Costessey; and the Norwich Dairy Farmers' Association, which asked the public to "use more milk for healthy children". The only national advertisement in the roll is for the Huddersfield Building Society. There is a notice by the advertising agents - "For space on this film apply Youngers, 34 Oxford Street, London"; the firm eventually became

Below: A typical local advertising slide. This was shown at the Southwold Cinema.

Pearl, Dean and Youngers. Finally "This Theatre is sprayed with Saville's June, England's most exquisite perfume". This was an air-freshener to help get rid of the smell of stale tobacco. These advertisements, which ran for about thirty seconds each, were very much like those in newspapers. They consisted usually simply of words, often animated - that is, writing themselves on the screen - and sometimes a drawing or a photograph or two. If a cameraman was employed to film some scenes the advertisement became a mini-film. Bonds, the Norwich department store, had an advertising film made in 1922 which ran, it is said,

This selection from the Bond's advertising film commences with a shot of the directors, followed by Miss George, the oldest employee, 44 years with the firm. 1920's bathing fashions follow. On the next page hats are modelled, we see customers being served and some of the displays.

for several years at the Thatched Cinema next door. The film starts with a photograph of Bonds first shop in 1879, when a branch of the Chelmsford firm set up business in the city. The directors of Bonds appear, rather self-consciously, and then Miss George, the longest-serving employee, who had been with the firm for forty-four years and is clearly not inclined to make any concessions to the camera. Some of Bonds' shop assistants model hats and coats and there are shots both inside and outside the store.

At the other end of the scale was the cinema advertisement shown nationally. The Norwich firm of J. and J. Colman made publicity history when they launched "The Mustard Club" advertising campaign on September 28th, 1926, the first advertisements appearing on London buses asking simply "Has Father Joined the Mustard Club?" People were intrigued and newspapers commented. This was followed by pictures of the Mustard Club members - The Baron de Beef, Miss Di Gester, Lord Bacon of Cookham, Signor Spaghetti, Lady Hearty and Master Mustard. A recipe book of the Mustard Club appeared with rules, that every member must eat mustard with snacks and meals, and that fellow eaters should be encouraged to do likewise. The recipe book and the campaign were the product of advertising agency S.H. Benson, "practitioners in advertising, experts in propaganda".

Working on the campaign and writing most of the copy was Dorothy L. Sayers, author of the Lord Peter Wimsey detective stories. The recipe book was written jointly by Dorothy Sayers and her husband, Oswald Atherton Flemming, with some additional recipes from Cottington Taylor of the Good Housekeeping Institute. There are seventy recipes, from steamed kippers to pigs' trotters, from Walnut Ketchup to Grandmother's Bacon Fraze, and there is a chapter on vegetarian dishes. Naturally every recipe lists mustard as one of the ingredients.

A series of cinema advertising films, running about six minutes each, was produced as part of the campaign. "The Mustard Club Topical Budget" was a spoof newsreel in which The Baron de Beef lays a foundation stone with mustard cement; Master Mustard wins a race and receives his prize - a mustard pot; Lord Bacon is seen in training for boxing and having a mustard bath; and finally the Mustard Club's annual banquet is covered.

One of these advertising films, "The Order of the Bath", concerns a man with a streaming cold whose wife gives him a reviving drink and orders him to join the Mustard Club. He falls asleep and dreams that the officers of the Mustard Club come

A scene from the Order of the Bath, one of the Mustard Club films, made for Colmans by Publicity Films as part of the Mustard Club campaign run by Bensons Advertising Agency.

to life and discuss his application. Witnesses for the prosecution are called, a ham sandwich and a wedge of cheese, who state that the defendant eats without mustard. They order him to have a mustard bath. He wakes up, has a mustard bath and enjoys a meal - with mustard!

The Mustard Club campaign was extremely successful. J. & J. Colman set up a special Mustard Club office to deal with the work of sending out badges (at its peak 2,000 applications for badges, priced at threepence each, were received every day), and answering letters. There were Mustard Club songs, books, fancy dress costumes, postcards, and even a card game. The Mustard Club advertising campaign ran for seven years, closing in March, 1933.

Another type of advertising short was the publicity film. The National Progress Film Company, formed in the 1930s to make advertising and sponsored films, made films about health and road safety. It

A wedge of cheese is about to give evidence against the defendant who did not use mustard.

also made a couple of films publicising the delights of Yarmouth as a holiday resort, "Eastern Sunshine" and "Sunshine, Fun and Laughter" both being made in the same year by Albert Arch, featuring personalities of the time.

In "Eastern Sunshine", British star Jack Hobbs arrives by aeroplane at Yarmouth, where he meets Dodo Watts. The couple wander round the town, taking in the sights, strolling through gardens, having a go on the dodgems and looking at the boating lake, where a distracted oarsman rows straight into the bank. They visit the races and go dancing at the Wellington Pier Winter Gardens, while both of them keep up a continuous dialogue over shots of themselves and general views of places and activities. The film was shot silent and the dialogue recorded later in the studio, with music mixed in. After riding in a speedboat and watching a concert party at the Wellington Pier, Jack Hobbs says over shots of a firework display,

A scene from "Eastern Sunshine", a 1933 film advertising the delights of Yarmouth; here featuring a promotion at the Wellington Pier.

"The wisest thing we have ever done is to come to Yarmouth". "It's the end of a perfect day", chips in Dodo. "It's the beginning of a perfect holiday", concludes Jack.

"Sunshine, Fun and Laughter" follows the same pattern, except that this time Kathleen Daw is the personality. Both films run for about ten minutes and, apart from the shots with the stars in, contain much the same material. In fact some shots have been duplicated and used in both films, while others have been cut in half with the beginning of a shot in one film and the second half in the other. Unlike "Eastern Sunshine", "Sunshine, Fun and Laughter" has a commentary spoken by Leonard Caplan, with occasional lines from Miss Daw. One sequence was shot from the top of the revolving tower (this 150ft structure was demolished in 1941), with Kathleen Daw in the foreground and the Marine Parade and the sands below, with people moving around looking like ants. "Every

Above: The peanut seller from "Great Yarmouth for Health, Sunshine, Pleasure".

of children and adults in fancy dress, ready for the carnival, including an orientally-dressed man selling "London roasted peanuts" from a barrow. The caption introducing him says "this seller of peanuts must have been 'sum knut from Pekin'!" Following scenes of the children's playground and the swimming pool, we are shown bags of salt being loaded on to a drifter at the quayside, and then a sequence taken from a Pathe Pictorial sub-titled "Sunday, A Yarmouth Study. The 7th day and stray boats of the great fishing fleet are returning to harbour". This section was obviously spliced in at a later date for it was not filmed until 1929.

In this sequence a Yarmouth drifter, YH 365, named "Oak Apple", steams into harbour to join what seems to be an endless line of boats moored upriver. "On the quayside, the men whose toil combs the North Sea are resting - in their Sunday best", says a title as we are shown groups of

inch of it a holidaymaker's paradise", says Leonard Caplan, and to this Miss Daw replies in perfect synchronisation "marvellous". This would have been recorded in the studio as the silent picture was projected on the screen - a method known as post-synchronisation.

Albert H. Arch photographed and directed both films. His enthusiasm for using his best shots twice resulted in Kathleen Daw turning up unrecognised and unmentioned in "Eastern Sunshine"!

These were not the first publicity films made for the town, for ten years earlier "Great Yarmouth for Health, Sunshine, Pleasure", a silent film partly in colour, had been made. The unknown maker of this started with shots from the revolving tower (the top platform ceased to revolve in 1915, but it was still known as the revolving tower), then concentrated on views of the Marine Parade and

Below: Healthy visitors at Yarmouth from the film "Great Yarmouth for Health, Sunshine, Pleasure".

Above: Loading salt on to a drifter at Yarmouth, from "Great Yarmouth for Health, Sunshine, Pleasure".

fishermen standing around talking. These were probably the visiting Scottish fishermen who had followed the herring down the coast, for the Norfolk men had no reservations about fishing on a Sunday.

The final section of "Health, Sunshine, Pleasure" is in colour, and shows various postcard type views of the resort. There is the beach crowded with holidaymakers, the swimming pool, model boating lake, Nelson's Column, the Cenotaph and its gardens, the harbour, Gorleston beach and Caister Castle, all awash in gentle colours added after the film had been made.

Stencil colour, or Pathe colour as it was known, had been around since 1905 as a method of colouring existing black and white films. The prints to be coloured were sent to the Pathe factory at Vincennes in France, where a small army of women was employed to make the stencils. Each

frame of the film (there are sixteen frames to a foot of 35mm film, and in the silent days a foot of film lasted exactly one second) was inspected, and a pointer delicately moved around the area or areas to be coloured with one hue. The pointer activated a cutting mechanism that produced a hole in a blank piece of film in direct relation to the area scanned by the pointer. All parts of the frame for red were traced and cut, and then the process was repeated for blue areas and again for yellow. The finished stencils would then be run on a special machine that brought the black and white prints in contact with the stencils and aniline dyes would be applied to the film through the cut-out sections of the stencils by rollers. By putting one colour on top of the other various mixtures and tones were obtained.

Stencil colour was usually used for areas of a picture rather than for individual parts. Trees with

Above: Blickling Hall, near Aylsham, in Norfolk, from a stencil colour film.

foliage were green all over, roofs were a red colour and the sky blue. When stencil colour was used well the results were very pleasing. If, however, it was done too quickly the colours were not accurately superimposed and sometimes became unsteady. In a stencil colour film of Blickling Hall, made in 1929 when this seventeenth century mansion was still a private home, in a long shot of the house and gardens the green colour does not cover the lawn adequately, but keeps hovering on the edge, leaving sometimes green grass, sometimes black and white grass.

Commercial firms or advertising agencies occasionally hired cinemas and village halls for film shows advertising products they were promoting, admission was, of course, free. A film was made of a particular product - usually showing its manufacture - and hand bills were distributed inviting the audience to a morning or afternoon show. As recently as 1963 a Danish firm hired the Regal in North Walsham, where a small audience saw a 35mm colour sound film extolling the advantages of pressure cookers.

In 1931 Chivers and Sons Ltd., of Histon near Cambridge, used this method of presentation for their ambitious sixty-minute film "From the Orchard to the Home", which proudly showed off this famous and successful family firm and its products. Now it provides a valuable record of factory life and processes.

The Chivers family, fruit farmers in the middle of the 19th century, sent their produce to market as well as distributing it from their own depot in Bradford. Finding that their best customers were jam makers, the Chivers decided to have a go at making their own jam, and the first boiling took place in a barn at Impington, Cambridgeshire, in 1873. The venture was so successful that Stephen Chivers and his sons were able to expand the business by buying an orchard close to Histon railway station and building the Victoria Works, opened in 1875. Ten years later a hundred and fifty people worked there, and by 1894 the workforce had increased to four hundred.

Chivers introduced table jellies in 1888, followed by custard powder, lemon curd, mincemeat, Christmas puddings and "Old English Marmalade". They renamed the works the Orchard Factory in 1910 and a year later received the Royal Warrant as purveyors of jams, jellies and canned English fruits.

In 1906 pioneer film maker, R.W. Paul, went to Histon and made a four-minute film, "Jam Making", which showed women picking currants, the jam boilers at work and the business of putting jam into pots and labelling. It is not clear whether this film was an "interest" film made by Paul to be included in his own catalogue or whether it was an advertising film commissioned by Chivers. Both types of films were being made at this time. Glenn Horridge in his "The Growth and Development of a Family Firm" mentions an advertising film, "The Chivers Story", made in 1908 by the London Bioscope Company; this could have been a new film or the earlier one reissued with a new title.

Neither of these films have survived, but the 1931 film "From the Orchard to the Home" has. This silent film, which was accompanied by a representative when shown, opens with scenes at the Chivers farms, which covered almost eight thousand acres. We are shown, with informative captions, the orchards, the beehives ("necessary in fertilising the fruit blossom, also for honey for use in Orchard Factory"), free-range chickens ("for eggs for lemon curd and mayonnaise"), two

Top: The opening title of a 1931 publicity film of Chivers jam and jelly factory at Histon, Cambridgeshire.

2: Horses on one of the Chivers Farms being shown off for the camera.

3: Free-range chickens on one of the Chivers Farms at Histon.

Bottom: Part of the huge store where the jars of jam were stored to cool.

Top right: The final job in producing jam at Chivers was to wrap the jars in tissue paper.

6: Packing cartons of jellies into boxes.

7: Loading cans of peas into "crates" prior to cooking.

Bottom right: The surgery was just one part of the welfare services provided for the workers at Histon.

thousand pedigree pigs ("fed on waste from factory and fallen fruit") and sheep, cows and Percheron horses which "are used on all the Chivers farms".

Because of its historical content it is worth examining the film more closely. The process of making jam is followed in detail - raspberries and strawberries are picked, weighed and taken to the Orchard Factory by horse-drawn waggons. The open boxes of fruit "to be used either for jam, fruit canning or pressed to provide fruit juices for jellies" are unloaded at the factory by Chivers employees, who seem extremely busy. Clean overalls, extra hands, often pretty girls and the obvious presence of a supervisor or two all have to be looked for and taken into account when watching films made in factories and works. The boss or someone from "public relations" was often present when a film camera was at work, making sure that everything looked right and that employees were working hard.

The fruit for jam is tipped by hand into silver-lined boiling pans, and the correct amount of sugar is added automatically. Glass jars arriving at the unloading bay are individually inspected and washed before being put on a conveyor and filled automatically with jam. Rows of women nimbly put discs of waxed paper on top of the still-warm jam, the lids are put on by hand, and the jars of jam go through a sterilizer and vacuum chamber.

The Orchard Factory had an extensive tramline system carrying hand-pushed trolleys for conveying the jam to and from the huge cooling rooms. This transport system, complete with points and sidings, was used by the film maker for a tracking shot inside the store to show the smartly dressed women unloading and stacking the jars of jam for cooling. The tramline system, built into the original factory in 1875, continued in use until 1939.

In the labelling and packing department the jars of jam are seen being polished by hand, and then string is tied round the tops to secure the lids and a coding machine ensures that "every individual jar can be traced throughout its career". After the label is put on, the jars are wrapped in tissue paper, again by hand, and boxed.

Chivers were the first to introduce transparent jelly in concentrated block form that could be made up at home. The process of making the jelly tablets is shown in detail in the film with shots of the fruit being pressed, the jelly being strained through muslin cloths and allowed to settle in trays. The cooled jelly is cut up by the cubing machine, wrapped neatly by hand and packed into cardboard boxes.

Stringless beans, carrots, celery hearts, peas, spinach, new potatoes and tomatoes were just some of the canned vegetables and fruit marketed by Chivers under the Gold Standard, 'English Grown' label; all picked and packed the same day. In 1931 a new factory was opened at Huntingdon for canning only, and the pea canning section of "From the Orchard to the Home" was probably shot there. The process of canning is covered in detail, with sequences showing the peas being picked by hand and arriving in sacks at the factory by lorry. The pea canning is much more automated than any other operation seen in the film. The "wonderful pea-shelling machines" are shown, as well as another piece of equipment which removes "small, immature and large over-ripe peas". Chivers were obviously proud of their canning machines which "fill and seal 120 cans per minute!" but much of the work was still done by hand. The cans were placed by women into large metal baskets called crates, which were loaded by block and tackle into large retorts. After cooking and cooling the cans are seen being taken out of the crates by hand. "The same care and cleanliness are predominant in the packing of all Chivers canned vegetables", says a caption that is followed by a wide shot of about a hundred women seated at trestles, each with a bowl, peeling and preparing vegetables for canning.

This 1931 film gives us a great deal of general information about Chivers and its products. Crates of jam and marmalade are rolled before the camera to show us the extent of Chivers trading - Hong Kong, Colombo, Montreal, Antwerp, New York, Jerusalem, Alexandria, Brussels, The Hague, Takoradi and Mombassa. The Histon laboratories in which the ingredients for Chivers products were tested are shown. In the kitchens, where foods are tried out, a young lady gingerly pokes a jelly to see how wobbly it is. At the railway sidings there is a great deal of activity (specially for the film camera?) loading boxes and crates into railway wagons, and we also see similar scenes of loading the Chivers fleet of vans and lorries.

In 1931 about three thousand people were employed on the Chivers farms and at the Histon factory. The film points out that the welfare of the staff was not overlooked, taking us into the large canteen where staff could get food at cost price, the surgery, a girls' recreation ground and to Impington Hall, a sixteenth-century building where "educational classes for all employees under eighteen years of age are held during working hours". The cameraman filmed the Chivers workers coming out of the factory at lunchtime, a shot that is reminiscent of the Lumiere film of 1895, and he could not resist taking a shot of the old barn where the first jam was made by Stephen Chivers in

Holidaying on the Broads in the 1920's - a frame from one of the "Beauty Spots of Britain" series.

1873, contrasting this with aerial views of the extensive factory layout in 1931. The name Chivers still appears on marmalades and jellies, although the factory at Histon was taken over by Schweppes in 1959.

Travel and scenic films were an ingredient of cinema programmes from time to time. In the mid-1920s H.E. Hayward and cameraman Frank Canham filmed idyllic scenes on the Norfolk Broads for the Royalty series "Beauty Spots of Britain". The shots, of beautiful quality, show Wroxham Broad, Belaugh and Coltishall. At Horstead there's the mill, Heggatt Hall, and "Little Switzerland" - disused marl pits that were a picturesque feature of the Norfolk Broads years ago. The film, consisting of straight shots without much action in them, goes on to show Salhouse Broad, Woodbastwick Old Hall and the old inn at Horning Ferry.

This film went the rounds of the cinema, but twenty-five years later another film of the Broads failed to make it. Victor Harrison, a cine enthusiast and Broads lover who owned a chain of cinemas in East Anglia which included the Regal Cinemas in Aylsham, Cromer, Stowmarket and North Walsham and the Ritz, Capitol, Norvic and Carlton in Norwich as well as two cinemas at Walton-on-the-Naze, decided to make a documentary about the Broads. Director/cameraman Riccy Smith was engaged and, under the working title "White Wings", over 1,000ft of 35mm film was shot; then for some reason the project came to an abrupt halt. The film was never completed and the nitrate rushes were left in a can for many years.

From this unedited material and from some short sequences taken on 16mm film by Victor Harrison in the 1930s, "The Broads Remembered" has been compiled - a nostalgic look back at the Broads with commentary by Nat Bircham, a former wherry skipper. Riccy Smith's shots of Wroxham include interior and exterior views of Roys - known even then as "The world's largest village store" - before modernisation, and a sequence of Horstead mill with water wheel and machinery working. Horstead mill was gutted by fire one freezing night in the winter of 1963, and this compilation film includes some views of the smouldering remains taken the next morning.

Nat Bircham leads us gently through the film, remembering the good old days and talking about his working life on the Broads. "I have had a wonderful life; very, very hard, I remember they

Horstead Mill, exterior and interior, and the undershot wheel which drove two pairs of stones.

say the good old days, but they weren't good old days really, but I enjoyed it. I remember in 1928, when I was first married, I was all alone on a wherry carting sugar beet. I had a very hard winter that one. I used to get 25/3d a freight cartage (£1.26p) I had to load it by hand, used to get tuppence a ton for loading them, used to have to wheel them sometimes 30 or 40 feet across the road to get them on board, but the total money I got was 25/3d a freight to Cantley. I used to do two a week and my average hours for 1928 - I've got records of it somewhere - I was working seven days a week, eighteen hours a day on average, and I should think my money was about fourpence or something an hour, piecework. Every time I had to go up the river I had to take the keel off because it drawed too much water, then when I got below Ludham Bridge, I had to fiddle about and get the keel back on. It would take me hours and my hands would be blooming numb."

Above: Equipment for drainage bank repairs in "Charted Waters" made in 1943.

During the 1940s three films were made about the Fens. In 1943 Widgey Newman, who made short general interest films for the cinema, set off with his wife Joan and cameraman Roy Plaskitt to make "Charted Waters", a light, humorous but interesting look at the fen region. Shot mainly in the Ely area, the film follows no theme or structure but is just a collection of sequences and shots linked by a whimsical commentary, delivered at break-neck speed. In fact it is a typical cinema interest short of a type which is forgotten today, but was expected by cinema audiences in the 1930s and 1940s as part of the "full supporting programme".

"Charted Waters" is unusual in that it was made in wartime and Widgey Newman's commentary, which was there to enliven the visuals and entertain the audience with funny remarks, is at times topical. Over shots of some swans taking to the air from a narrow waterway the commentary runs "Mr and Mrs Swan take off down the new cut, called New because it was only built in 1232. On some maps it's called Ye Olde Cut - not meaning your pre-war meat portion, and no relation to two veg."

This three reeler (a reel of 35mm film is 1,000ft long and runs for about ten minutes) begins with sequences of drainage channel bank repairs, steam pumping engine houses and George Turner's blacksmith's shop with twin forges at Brandon Creek, between Southery and Littleport. Eel nets and traps are seen at Prickwillow, and at Ely willow canes are prepared for basket making. "First they are stacked after which, having been allowed to season - August is the best season for this job - they are put into water to soak until they are as supple as Carmen Miranda's hips. They are kept under water, the willows of course, not the Brazilian bombshell's lumbar regions, until they are ready to get thoroughly het up." Over shots of the rods being boiled, Widgey Newman's commentary continues "Here's Albert getting the hetting ready and making sure they are all cooked to a turn. When they are cooked they turn without breaking". Albert is seen twisting the rods to see if they are bendy enough for the basketmaker.

Mr Hunt, the last basketmaker in Ely, is then seen making what the commentary describes as a shopping basket but looks more like a potato basket. Following some shots at the Fish and Duck Inn at the junction of the River Ouse and the old West River at Little Thetford, where a customer plays skittles, Widgey Newman and his crew take to a small boat in search of otters. Widgey Newman had made several films in the 1930s about animals, but this sequence proved more difficult than the zoo subjects and horses that he was used to. First the outboard motor propeller becomes tangled with weeds, so they have to walk across Hemingford fens to set up their hide. Eventually some otters are seen, but the shots look suspiciously as though they have been borrowed from another film. Anyway, one of the film crew sneezes and all that is left are ripples on the water. After sequences at Huntingdon, Littleport, Holywell, Over and St. Ives, Widgey Newman returns to Ely to see a cooper at Hall, Cutlack and Harlock's brewery, making a barrel and to show off the splendours of the Cathedral. "Charted Waters" was released early in 1944, the year Widgey Newman died - aged 44.

In 1945 Greenpark Productions made "Fenlands" - a film mainly to do with farming in the fens for the Ministry of Information. It was number four in a series of films under the collective title "The Pattern of Britain". The other three dealt with farming in Leicestershire, Sutherland and Cornwall. "Fenlands" shows the type of crops the area is best suited to growing, together with the problems of reclamation. The message of the film is how man has conquered the area and that through hard work the ordinary land worker can build up a small-holding and achieve success and satisfaction. Directed by Ken Annakin it is a well made and interesting film, but it does not fall into the commercial film category.

In 1947 a film crew spent three days at Mepal, in the Cambridgeshire fens not far from Ely, where the typical fenman's home of Alfred Wilson at Low Bank shows how self-supporting the fenman was, with his beehives, pig in a pigsty and a plantation of willows which he used for making eel traps. The newly made traps, three-foot-long cigar-shaped pipes called hives or grigs, have to be submerged for about a week to become waterlogged before they are ready for use. Alfred Wilson and John Waters demonstrate in the film how the traps are laid at intervals in a channel and also how an eel net is laid across the dyke in a horseshoe shape, kept in place by the flow of water. The net has a long hooped funnel in the middle which traps the eels. The next morning the traps are recovered and emptied and the ends of the funnel net lifted and the contents slipped into a bucket. The eels, kept alive in a submerged chest, are weighed and boxed when the buyer visits the fenman's home.

John Waters laying an eel net in a fen channel, from "An English Fen".

Called "An English Fen", this two-reeler made by British Foundation Pictures, was directed and edited by Ronald Haines (this apparently was not his real name - he was in fact W.R. Hutchinson), who made one mistake when writing the straight-forward, informative commentary - an error that makes local audiences today roar with laughter as the film opens with the line "In the heart of Lincolnshire, on a little hill, rises the tall and graceful edifice - Ely Cathedral".

Some Visiting Film Makers

"Drifters", released in 1929, a film of the herring fisheries, sparked off the documentary film movement in this country. What is seldom realised is that most of the film was shot off the East Anglian coast, and in the towns of Great Yarmouth and Lowestoft.

In the spring of 1928 John Grierson, who is credited with being the first to coin the word "documentary", although the word "documental" had already been used, joined the Empire Marketing Board as an assistant film officer. The aim of the government-financed board was the promotion of trade, and Grierson's first job was to make them a film. The board wanted a film on the herring fleets, so Grierson travelled to Lerwick in the Shetlands and started work with cameraman Basil Emmott, filming local scenes, some birds and some shots aboard a local drifter, the Maid of Thule.

Attempts made in the Shetlands to film the actual catching of herrings were not successful, and Grierson and Emmott came down to East Anglia and went filming on the Lowestoft drifter "Renoulle".

"Drifters" opens with views of fishermen's cottages intercut with shots of gulls and seas breaking. There is much intercutting and quick cutting in places - this Grierson, who edited the film himself, learnt from the pace and montage of some Russian films he had seen a year or two earlier. Some of the short shots taken in the Shetlands are mixed with the East Anglian material, though these soon become obvious. There are no outcrops of rock off the East Anglian coast and the bearded skipper of the "Maid of Thule" is quickly identifiable.

At the fishing grounds the nets are shot and the crew go below. The interior shots of the crew's

John Grierson and Basil Emmott preparing to shoot a scene for "Drifters". (Photo: National Film Archive, London)

quarters were filmed on a specially constructed set while John Grierson and Basil Emmott were at Lerwick. What appear to be underwater scenes of herring swimming into the nets are completely faked. Not only were these sequences done in a tank at the marine laboratories at Plymouth, but apparently the fish are not herring at all, but roach! It seems that herring could not be caught and kept alive in a tank, so a substitute had to be found.

The crew turn out and the nets are hauled. The intercutting of hands on nets, ropes, the throbbing engine and the funnel give the impression of long, hard work and of the toil involved in catching herring.

"Despite the help of the winch every foot has to be fought for". More titles inform us that it takes eight hours to haul 150 crans, and that there are a thousand herrings to a cran. The returning boats head for Lowestoft or Yarmouth, where the catch is unloaded. Most of the sequences of landing herring were filmed at Yarmouth, for the swills, those strange double baskets peculiar to the town, give the place away. The distinctive quayside buildings also help identify the location.

Next the catch is gutted by the fishergirls and then boxed and barrelled. Finally there is a sequence of railway fish trucks, probably not filmed in East Anglia, taking the herring away.

Two other films made for educational purposes were constructed out of the material Grierson and Emmott shot. They are "Our Herring Industry", which is a shorter, more straightforward version of the herring story, and "Drifting", which concentrates on the actual drift-net procedure.

In 1938 two young film technicians, Joseph Valentine Durden and Brian Salt, drove around East Anglia collecting material for a film on windmills. They were just two of the many film-makers who visited the region in the 1930s and 40s, either because East Anglia offered the subject they wanted to film or merely because it was convenient and they liked the place. Joe Durden was a biologist writing and directing films for Gaumont British Instructional Films, while Brian Salt specialised in animation, shooting the many animated diagrams that appeared in much of this firm's output.

Using "short ends", cheaply bought unexposed leftovers from the feature film industry, and Joe's Newman Sinclair clockwork 35mm camera, the pair filmed the different types of windmills then working. The film traces the development of windmills from the small post mill at Bourne, near Cambridge, to a smock mill at Herringfleet, where

Herringfleet smock mill, used for draining the marshes.

Charlie Howlett, in a detailed sequence, is seen winching the cap round into the wind and preparing the cloth sails for work. Then at Soham Mere a large smock mill is shown, followed by a tower mill at Haverhill, with its unique circular sail. A diagram illustrating the internal workings of windmills is followed by shots of gear wheels and stones at work. This well-made film ends with a sequence of other devices that use wind-power, such as gliders, kites and yachts. A good informative commentary was added, spoken by Carlton Hobbs, who was responsible for most of the Gaumont British commentaries, and a short piece of music was overlaid at the beginning and end. "And Now They Rest", as this film was titled, was made by two enthusiastic film-makers for whom film-making was an end in itself; it was not until the film was completed that they thought about distribution. The large distributors like United Artists and MGM only dealt with short films made by themselves or associated companies. For the independent producer it was better to go to one of the smaller

Charlie Howlett at Herringfleet smock mill.

distributors, and Durden and Salt went to Exclusive Films. Today Joseph Durden and Brian Salt's film is sought after by the windmill enthusiast as some of the mills seen at work have long since disappeared.

Earlier the same year, on February 13th, a northerly gale accompanied by high spring tides resulted in the sea bursting through the sand hills at Horsey, in east Norfolk. This unremembered flood, which covered 15 square miles of low lying countryside, was filmed by Pathe Gazette, whose camera crew rushed down and took some aerial shots and scenes of flooded fields to make a 19 shot sequence for their newsreel.

This local flood was also recorded by Patrick Jackson of the G.P.O. film unit, who made an eight minute film centring on the people who continued working regardless of the water - the postmen. Claude Simmonds, the local postman, and Bob O'Brian, a Yarmouth post van driver, are the real stars of this film. The commentary informs us that Claude normally has a two mile daily delivery, but because of the flooded coast road he has to make a 15 mile detour. Bob O'Brian, brought in to drive Claude to work, then takes over the commentary and, in a jolly Norfolk accent, comments on things they see as they drive along. When a submerged car is spotted with just its roof showing, Bob tells us that the owner spent 15 hours on top of it before being rescued, and that a submerged tractor in a field only recently cost the farmer "200 quid".

After emptying his boots of water, Claude falls into a boat and is rowed to a remote farm. Here he is given a cup of tea. "What, more tea? Old Claude must be half full of tea by now", says Bob. The film ends with a small army of labourers doing their best to repair the gap in the sandhills, and the final line of commentary tells us that "until the roads are clear again Claude has to row six miles every day to deliver the Horsey mail."

It is a gentle and amusing film, reminding us of one of those coastal incidents that are so often quickly forgotten.

During the war Richard Massingham made a film of student life at Cambridge. Called simply "Cambridge", the film follows the daily life of undergraduates - at lectures, at practical work, and relaxing in the convivial atmosphere of the town. Filmed towards the end of the war, it is interesting for its scenes of A.R.P, and A.F.S. practice around the colleges. Eight years later, in 1952, Richard Dimbleby visited Norwich to look at Caley's chocolate factory, Colman's mustard works and other industries for "Come with me to Norwich", a film probably intended to be the first in a series of visits to prominent English towns and cities, although no other film with a "Come with me" prefix seems to have been made.

Many film makers who visited East Anglia came here for its farming or its associated country life. And it is because of them that so much of the region's rural life has been preserved on film. In the late 1930s Marion Grierson, John Grierson's sister, and Evelyn Spice, a Canadian journalist turned film maker, visited north Essex to make a film that showed that the English village, very much connected with agriculture, was neither backward nor out of touch with the world as people might think. "Around the Village Green", made for the Travel and Industrial Development Association, with music by Benjamin Britten, shows how the English village, in this case Finchingfield, was changing in line with the towns.

After haymaking and harvest scenes we are shown round the village, with shots of the petrol station, a telephone box, the arrival of a bus, the postman on his round and some shops and modern bungalows.

Outside the Fox public house an old man speaks of his satisfied life. He tells us he pays three shillings (15p) a week for his cottage. "I've got a radio, and a gramophone, and I haven't got a bath, but I've got a river down the bottom of the garden, so I have a good bath when I want one." He goes on to comment, "But they have a better time in the village than when I was a boy, I used to walk one and a half miles to work and get one-and-six (7½p) frightening crows off the parson's field."

A similar theme was followed by director Darrel Catling in "Lowland Village", filmed in and around Lavenham in 1942. Produced by Gaumont British Instructional Films, this shows the daily routine of village life and how it is dependent on the surrounding land. To set the scene there are some shots of the smaller village of Kersey, then the architecture of Lavenham is briefly mentioned in a sequence that explores the past prosperity of the village. Some shots here of a weaver at a loom, of spinning, and of some silk cloth may have been borrowed from another film, but they are included here to illustrate past trades. Then the film launches into its day in the life of Lavenham. Early morning shots show farm labourers walking to walk, the milkman and postman on their rounds, the children going off to school. "After they have taken the younger children to school", runs the commentary, "the mothers and womenfolk do their shopping, but there's always time for a chat before getting down to the day's housework." And here we see women at upstairs windows chatting across the street - an intriguing trick of the film maker, as those who know Lavenham well realise that the dormer windows shown are not in fact opposite each other. Cows, having been milked, wander along Water Street, and then the film dwells on the farming year. Here there are scenes of harvest, sugar beet lifting, winter hedging and ditching, and spring ploughing and drilling.

Farm workers going off to work in Lavenham for the 1942 film "Lowland Village".

A sequence described in the commentary as village craftsmen "attending to what might be called the farmer's equipment" shows Mr Huffey, the blacksmith in Water Street, and Mr Bullivant, the saddler in the High Street. The last-named, who had a sign over his shop "There's Nothing Like Leather", put on his prize medals for the filming as he worked on a hand-sewn harness. A wheelwright is also shown, and the commentary continues "Thus these trades, unchanging with the years, keep alive a tradition of the past, while serving the needs of the farmer today." Like "Around the Village Green", the Lavenham film is quick to point out that the village does not lag behind the progress of the towns. Gas, piped water and electricity are all used in the village. Trains and new roads provide transport. "During the centuries the village has seen many changes, but has survived them all." The inhabitants "foregather at the inn and in true democratic fashion, discuss their politics and air their views"; over this we see a man drinking beer out of a glass boot!

As for recording activities on the land, there are films in the Archive from almost every decade. "Village in the Wheatfields", made in Rickinghall in 1949, shows village life and work on the land throughout the seasons; in 1966 Hugh Brandon-Cox recorded on a Cambridge farm the activities during winter and spring; and in the 1970s

Boulton Hawker Films issued "A Farm in East Anglia", filmed at Elmsett, near Hadleigh, showing the season's work on a Suffolk farm. But possibly the best and most comprehensive set of films covering the farming year are "Farming in Autumn", "Farming in Winter", "Farming in Spring" and "Farming in Summer", filmed on two farms in East Suffolk during the farming year of 1934. These two farms were Wood Farm at Sibton near Peasenhall, a heavy-land holding of about 120 acres tenanted by Mr Floyd Peecock, and a combination of light-land farms near Leiston known as St.Mary's Abbey Farm, Lower Abbey Farm and Upper Abbey Farm. The tenant here was Arthur Rope, then in his 85th year, although the day to day management of the 1,000 acres, farmed as a single unit, was in the hands of his son, Mr G.A. Rope.

"Farming in Autumn" deals with carting beans, harvest-time, cutting maize, lifting sugar beet, making sheepfolds and autumn ploughing. The harvest sequence, filmed at Sibton, is particularly well covered. First two men scythe round the edge of the field to make way for the binder, then one of them ties the loose wheat with a straw bond, a length of straw wrapped round the wheat and neatly twisted to hold it together. The binder, pulled by three horses, goes round the field and the sheaves are stood up in shocks, stooks or traves, depending on what part of East Anglia you come from.

The corn is carted, and a stack is made and thatched to keep the weather out. It will be thrashed out in the winter months. The sugar beet crop is harvested by hand. The beet are pulled up using a knife with a small hook on the end, and knocked together to get the earth off, and then the leaves are chopped off. These will be used for cattle feed. The beet are put into heaps, then heaved by hand into a horse-drawn tumbril which takes its load to a convenient point by a gate where the contents are tipped out and loaded by hand again into a large waggon to be taken to the railway station.

There was an enormous amount of physical work in all farming jobs, although it is a bit of a surprise to see a bowler-hatted gentleman on a Fordson tractor ploughing up the stubble.

"Farming in Winter" opens with thrashing at Upper Abbey Farm. The tackle used, which belonged to the farm, consisted of a Garrett portable steam engine and a 1917 vintage Garrett drum, with an elevator made by E.R. & F. Turner of Ipswich. The old-fashioned portable engine continued in use until the Second World War, and the thrashing tackle on into the 1950s.

Scenes from the threshing sequence at Upper Abbey Farm, Leiston, from the 1934 film "Farming in Winter".

Throughout these films equipment and tools are seen in the hands of men who used them all the time. Today, they can only be seen hanging in museums or being shown at weekend events where traditional methods are demonstrated. The proper use of a cumbersome hay knife is seen when Mr Peecock at Sibton cuts slices of silage out of a stack to feed the cattle. "The silage has now set into a thick, solid mass, like plug tobacco, brown and juicy. It smells extremely strong but the cattle love it", says the commentator, Mr A.O.D. Claxton, who was deputy secretary for education in East Suffolk, an authority on the Suffolk dialect and "expert collaborator" for the films.

Back at Upper Abbey Farm, mangels, or cattle-beet as they were known, are taken from a clamp, an open-air storage heap covered with earth, for slicing and feeding to cattle. The mangels are fed by head stockman Lacey Smith into a root cutter driven by a Fairbanks Morse petrol engine. The roots and other ingredients are mixed together on the barn floor.

George Ewart Evans, author of "Ask the Fellows Who Cut the Hay" and other books about East Anglian country life, mentioned that bush draining goes back to pre-Roman times. On Mr Peecock's farm at Sibton, every detail of bush draining is shown in a sequence in "Farming in Winter". First the hedges are cut, and the best of the waste is kept. A network of trenches is dug across the field to be drained, using specially shaped tools as the trenches get deeper. Each of these tools is shown, sometimes in close-up, so that we can see how it worked. The bottom of the trench is smoothed with a curved tool which is also cupped, forming a channel along which the water runs. The brush-wood from the hedge is pressed into the trench just above the channel, preventing the earth from falling down and blocking the waterway when the trench is filled in. At the edge of the field, where the water runs into a ditch, two or three drainpipes are put in. For 2,000 years bush draining had been practised, but not any more; it exists now only on movie film. Finally in this section there is winter ploughing with a Ransomes YL horse-drawn plough.

"Farming in Spring" opens with the young cattle being let out of the yard and leaping for joy in a meadow with St.Mary's Abbey ruins in the back-ground. Some of Abbey Farms's thirty men then get to work. Mr Carey cleans out the yard, loading muck into a tumbril which is taken to a field where individual heaps of muck are made at regular intervals. Then it is spread by hand by Mr Spall, and Charlie Websdale, with a pair of horses and a Ransome's TCP plough, so called because at one stage of casting the steel is chilled, ploughs it in.

Bush draining at Wood Farm, Sibton, showing the different types of tools used. The sequence can hardly be described as startling, but it does provide a lasting record of an age-old technique.

In "Farming in Spring", after the cattle are let out of the yard when the warmer weather comes, the muck is cleared out and spread on the land and ploughed in. The scenes are at Upper Abbey Farm, Leiston.

The top frame shows the preparing of a seed bed for drilling. Grain is then tipped into a Smyth drill, and the three-man team commences work.

Back at the farm, Lacey Smith and Jack Ford prepare food for the sheep which is taken to the troughs and poured in by the head shepherd, Harry Self, and the sheep rush forward to eat. Will Walker is seen doing some spring ploughing, while Eddie Clarke shows how a sheepfold should be made out of wheat straw and branches from a hedge.

A drilling sequence shows a locally made Smyth drill, pulled by three horses and worked by three men, one to guide the drill by walking alongside operating the steering lever, one sitting on the seed box to look after the horses, and the third walking behind to make sure the grain was going down into the ground properly. Harrowing and rolling sequences follow, and then a remarkable demonstration of double-handed broadcasting by William Aldred of Poys Street, Sibton. Hand sowing of seed had virtually died out by this time, the method only being used for headlands, for the odd corners of fields, or for special seed or a top dressing of artificial manure. A tray of seed hung round the middle of the sower, and he walked along distributing the seed by picking a small amount out of the box with alternate hands. This was a very skilled job, depending on the rhythm of swinging the arms as the seed was spread, and walking in the right place. The broadcaster would never hear the end of it if he missed a bit. This would become evident when the crop first appeared, and then of course it was too late. The farmer who had a skilled broadcaster among his employees could count himself lucky.

Some of the nineteen sows then kept at Upper Abbey Farm are seen in "Farming in Summer" in a section dealing with the care of stock. Two old sheep shearers, the Palmer brothers of Kelsale, who were shearing contractors travelling around Suffolk, are seen at their trade, followed by a sequence of dipping ewes. A horse drawn hoe made by Garrett's of Leiston is seen hoeing through the new sugar beet crop, followed by "chopping out", as it was known in East Anglia. This is singling, with a hand hoe, a long back-aching job. The men move slowly across the field removing excess young beet, so as to leave a gap of about ten inches between each beet, thus enabling them to grow healthily. Chopping out is almost extinct now that monogerm seeds are commonplace. This means that a sugar beet seed, planted individually, produces one young beet at the prescribed distance from the next. A thick crop of oats, tares and beans at Sibton is cut for making into silage, followed by Floyd Peecock with tractor and mower cutting a rather thin crop of hay. A swath turner ensures that the hay dries properly, and finally the hay is made up into cocks as a precaution against rain.

The whole year's farming activities on a traditional English arable farm are seen in these four films. Apart from those relating to sugar beet, a relatively recent innovation, the farming processes depicted are virtually the same as they were in Queen Victoria's reign, with some methods going back hundreds of years. The work was done predominately by hand and animal power. Horses pulled machines that were made in local factories. James Smyth and Sons of Peasenhall made corn and seed drills; Richard Garrett in Leiston made farm implements, thrashing machines and traction engines, while at Ipswich Ransomes, Sims and Jefferies at the Orwell Works made rakes, potato diggers, cultivators, ploughs and thrashing tackle.

Agriculture was on the brink of change, much hastened by the Second World War. Traditionally run mixed farms growing crops and keeping livestock like Mr Peecock's survived into the 1950s, although he gave up Wood Farm at Sibton about 1939. The Abbey Farms at Leiston are now run by Richard Rope, grandson of Arthur Rope who came to the farm in 1870. In the mid 1930s about one man was required for every 33 acres, hence thirty men on Rope's 1,000 acre farm. Now it would be more like one man to 300 acres on an arable farm. Three of the men who worked on Rope's farm and one who was a boy at the time appear in a compilation film made in 1983 by the Film Archive. Jack Ford, Charlie Websdale and Herbert Smith talk about what it was like in those days.

Jack Ford remembers; "The farmer used to come out in the morning, the foreman used to see him and get the orders for the day. Then the foreman used to come up to the yard where we were, and give us all the orders to carry out. Stockmen, horsemen or anything used to have the day's orders. We used to do our best to carry out whatever he say." "It was seven o'clock in the morning till about half past four at night with a little time off for dinnertime" adds Herbert Smith. Charlie Websdale recounts "We used to have to depend on the old bike to get round the farm. When I was a'ploughing I used to ride the horse there, get off, and get to work, then take him and ride home."

They received 28 shillings a week (£1.40) and an extra £5 for getting the harvest in. They had Christmas Day, Boxing Day, Good Friday and Easter Monday off. The present shepherd, Leonard Button, was a boy when the films were made, and he remembers sheep shearing time, when his job was to fetch beer for the shearers. As fast as he collected it from the village, the shearers consumed it. The opportunity to record the original participants in such a film is rare, and a chance the Archive seized.

The original films were made by Mary Field for Gaumont British Instructional Films, and were intended for classroom use. Mary Field, with an M.A. from London University in Imperial History, became a film maker "quite by chance" after taking an interest in films during her academic studies.

British Instructional Films, formed in 1919 with Harry Bruce Woolfe at the helm, became famous for its "Secrets of Nature" films which it began making in 1922. Short films of about ten minutes each, these were studies of plant and animal life for cinema distribution, specialising in speeded up and slow motion. They were both successful and profitable.

In 1927 Mary Field joined Bruce Woolfe at British Instructional, and besides working on these films made others from ideas of her own. Bruce Woolfe, who had been trying to make educational films since 1911, had always wanted to make films for classroom use - hence British Instructional Films. But he found himself up against a lack of understanding on the part of both film makers and teachers on the use of film in the classroom, coupled with the fact that film and projectors cost money, of which there was precious little available.

In 1933, the problem was tackled by the Gaumont British Picture Corporation, which set up two companies, the first being Gaumont British Equipments, formed in July with the object of making 16mm and 35mm projectors available. "Suitable projection apparatus can be installed at shortest notice by means of the country-wide G.B.E. service organisation. Whether hired for the day, hire-purchased, or kept for use to be shared between schools and classrooms, one of the various portable models will be suitable for all individual needs. The GeBescope (16mm) projectors will show both sound and silent films at their correct speeds", said a Gaumont British advertisement for the time. In November, 1933, Gaumont British Instructional Films was organised with Harry Bruce Woolfe as director; at last he could do what he wanted, make films directly for classroom use. Mary Field moved over from British Instructional with him, and together they started work. Their main output in the 1930s consisted of films on biology, geography, hygiene, physical education and science, together with a new series of nature films entitled "Secrets of Life".

But Mary Field's greatest contribution during this time at G.B.I. must have been the series of films she made in Suffolk. It seems that soon after her appointment as a producer at G.B.I. in November, 1933, she travelled to East Anglia to make pre-

parations for her farming year films. Besides those featuring the four season she made four others, some by re-working the material she shot at Leiston and Sibton. One of them, "The Farm Factory", released in 1936, compared a farm, Upper Abbey Farm, with a factory. She showed with animated models that the farmyard, laid out in 1810 and still working efficiently in the 1930s, was thought out carefully and was not the haphazard set of buildings that it might at first seem. The structure of management of the farm is shown, with G.A. Rope at the head and his assistants, Lacey Smith, head stockman, Will Walker, head fieldsman, and Harry Self, head shepherd, underneath. They in turn had field hands to help them. The local community of Eastbridge is touched on with shots of the one pub, the Eel's Foot, and the one shop. The nearest school was at Theberton, one mile away, and children are seen walking and bicycling there. "School hours are dictated by the daylight", said the commentary," for the Eastbridge children must be home before the sun sets". Another of Mary Field's films, "Town Settlement", looks at Saxmundham, explaining with the aid of maps why peple settled there in the first place - mainly for geographical reasons.

"Wheatlands of East Anglia" uses parts of the farming year films plus other original sequences to look at wheat production. Again maps are used to show why East Anglia is particularly suitable for cereals. Sequences of Norwich Corn Hall in Exchange Street, Norwich Cattle Market, and Cole's Mill at Peasenhall help tell the story of what happens to wheat after the farmer has grown it.

But it is "This was England", a twenty-minute look at the continuous agricultural tradition existing in Suffolk from the Stone Age to the 20th century, which is the outstanding film of the set. Not only was it shown in selected cinemas but also to some special audiences of the time. It was viewed by members of the British Association for the Advancement of Science - something that was repeated nearly fifty years later when it was again shown to the British Association members in 1984 when the conference was held at the University of East Anglia. This time, however, it was for historical reasons, because it shows Suffolk industries that have survived only on film. "This was England" traces unbroken links with the past, the first sequence being of flint knapping at Brandon. The large flints are brought to the surface by the last of the flint miners, "Pony" Ashley, and flint knapper George Edwards then demonstrates his skill of making flints for use in old flintlock guns, and a round flint for building purposes.

George Edwards, flint-knapper.

The second sequence moves to farming. "The Ancient Britons used to farm my farm, and like me they found this heavy land holds the wet, and needs draining. They drained the land in a very simple way, and I do it the same way because it's cheap and it works all right" says Floyd Peecock, direct to the camera, in one of three sequences that start with the person involved telling us about their work. These sound shots were filmed in a studio with a background set to match the location surroundings. Mr Peecock is seen against a hedge which he turns to look at as he says "First of all we cut brushwood from the hedge", then the film cuts to the bush draining sequence seen in "Farming in Winter", re-edited. Again we see the laborious job of making a network of trenches across the field, the scraping out of the bottom of these with the special tools and the putting in of the brushwood. Finally we see water trickling through under the brushwood to show how the drain works. Making silage in a pit follows, with horses struggling with tumbrils up to the top of the heap, where the contents are tipped out.

The Anglo-Saxon period deals with broadcast sowing. Like the bush draining sequence, shots of William Aldred are re-worked to give a more detailed look at the art of broadcasting by hand. William Aldred's introduction gives an insight into his working life. In a warm Suffolk accent he says "In the olden times the Saxons used to broadcast all their corn and seed like this. In my young time I went to sea and was shipwrecked three times. Shipwrecked in the Sauce Pie off Yarmouth - a quarter of a mile off Yarmouth. The skipper come on deck and he said 'The mast and sails are over the side', he said, 'all hands on deck at once.' I've been a farming hand for forty years and I can sow seeds against anyone and I can sow ten acres of land with ten pints of seed."

The assistant gamekeeper on the Levett Scrivener estate at Sibton Abbey, "Brushey" Whincop, shows how to catch moles. Moles can be a great nuisance by throwing up heaps which make meadows and pastures uneven. It was quite common at one time to see the results of the mole catcher's efforts

William Aldred, broadcast sowing.

hanging on a barned wire fence, a row of bodies hung for all to see. "Brushey" Whicop demonstrates his art with self-springing traps made out of wood and wire. He too hangs his latest catch on the fence, and the camera pans round to show moles hanging on the wire almost as far as the eye can see.

Tudor England is associated with shipbuilding, and Mary Field shows us a Suffolk sawpit. This pit, at G.J.Aldridge's yard at Walpole, was in fact quite new. When George Aldridge moved his wheelwright, carpentry and undertaking business to the centre of Walpole, a new pit was dug in 1920. To demonstrate how a saw pit works George Aldridge, with assistant Billy Quinton, saws a tree trunk in half. The trunk is laid horizontally above the sawpit, enabling Mr Quinton to go down underneath to pull the saw down while George Aldridge stands on top of the trunk pulling the saw up. The job completed, the two halves roll apart as soon as the "dogs" are knocked out. These would then be cut individually into planks. Sawing was a slow business, but before steam engines and circular saws, all timber was cut in this way. The pit at Walpole was filled in in 1947, but the firm of Aldridge continues under the ownership of George's son Hubert Aldridge, although the day-to-day business in carried on by Hubert's son, Ralph Aldridge.

Ebenezer Joshua Rackham, straw and reed thatcher, also of Walpole, then takes up the story. He introduces us to a cottage that is about to be thatched with straw, which he helped his father to thatch thirty-six years before. The sequence that follows shows Ebenezer and his sons working on the cottage at Cookley, a small village not far from Walpole. Today there are Rackhams still working, Ebenezer's grandson Peter keeping up the family tradition.

"The 19th century saw Suffolk farmers taking to machinery", says the commentary, and here the thrashing sequence from "Farming in Winter", this time with authentic sound effects, is repeated.

Above: A gyrotiller at work somewhere in Suffolk from "This was England", for the sequence dealing with "Today"
Left: Ebenezer Joshua Rackham and sons thatching with straw.
Below: The sawpit at Walpole.

Above: ''Brushey'' Whincop, mole-catcher. Right: Floyd Peecock showing the correct usage of a silage cutting knife. Below: Floyd Peecock hedging at Wood Farm, Sibton.

From left to right: William Aldred, Mary Field, and Len Collins, manager of the Regent Cinema, Ipswich, where "This was England" was premiered on Sept. 7th 1935. Aldred received an ovation when he was seen on the screen.

Finally we see what is described as a 20th century machine - a gyrotiller. At that time it was thought that these huge crawling monsters, with revolving tines which dug into the ground doing the work of cultivator and plough, would become commonplace; in fact they proved too cumbersome. Mary Field's "This was England" is not recognised as a great film of the time, but it stands up well in comparison with the output of Grierson's rival documentary movement. Hers was a more subtle approach, documenting life as it was, without social comment or political undercurrents, presented simply and in a straightforward way. Her history background enabled her to recognise that the past had a place in the present.

In the handbook which accompanied the film she wrote "It is only too easy to forget in a mechanical age how even the latest methods of working have evolved from a long tradition of individual skills which can still be found with those who use local materials and methods in the more remote parts of the country. The development of communications and labour saving machinery during the last fifty years has speeded up the whole pace of everyday life and this film will more than fulfil the purpose for which it was made if it recaptures for those who see it, the natural and gentle pace of rural life adapted to the gradual changes of nature, and the careful and unhurried creation of individual work using simple hand tools and local materials. The Suffolk dialect, in which the men seen working explain how the various methods are used side by side, is rapidly disappearing and is therefore of special interest to the students of language."

Mary Field's use of sound is interesting. Sound films had been around for six years or so, but it was only in 1935 that sound was used to record ordinary people and what they had to say. "Workers and Jobs" used location sound as did "Housing Problems", both released in 1935, the same year as "This Was England". In "Housing Problems" audiences heard, direct from those who lived in the slums of London, what conditions were like. Today we are used to interviews in the street or home, but in 1935 this technique was revolutionary. Mary Field was well informed about the advances in film making, and she too used the direct camera technique in 1935. For all we know she may well have thought of it first - "This Was England" was made, as far as can be ascertained, between "Workers and Jobs" and "Housing Problems". Because of the lack of money, it was not possible to take the recording equipment and heavy cameras to remote parts of Suffolk. So Floyd Peecock, William Aldred and Ebenezer Rackham were recorded in a studio. And it worked well. Mr. Peecock speaks easily without any kind of hesitation or self-conciousness. Seventy-seven-year-old William Aldred speeds through his lines and at the end, almost before the last word is out, his eyes quickly move to one side, probably to Mary Field standing beside the camera, with a "was that all right?" look on his face. Ebenezer Rackham rests on a ladder, supposedly on the roof of the cottage at Cookley, which he is about to thatch. His piece to camera is a bit tense, and he appears to be putting on an exaggerated accent.

On Saturday 7th September 1935 "This Was England" was premiered at the Regent Cinema, now the Odeon, in Ipswich. Those who took part in the film and family and friends put on their best clothes and were taken by bus to the venue, about sixty of them in all. Undoubtedly the star of the occasion was William Aldred. "A roar of applause", it is recorded, went up from the audience when they saw him on the screen. He had never been to the cinema in his life before, and when asked what he thought of it he replied "I liked it wonderful well".

Recording East Anglian Life

It was the introduction of the smaller sized film gauges in the early 1920s that led to cine equipment and film becoming widely available at reasonably low cost for the non-professional user.

The real breakthrough, enabling these sub-standard gauges, as they were called, to succeed as home movie-making systems was the invention of reversably processed camera film. Until this time all black and white film was of the negative-positive type. A film could not be shown until a positive print had been made from the camera negative. Both the Kodak research laboratories in the United States and Charles Pathe laboratories in France produced an emulsion that could be processed to a direct positive as soon as it came out of the camera. As the processing was complicated, special laboratories were built to deal with this "Reversal" film as it was known, although the keen amateur could develop it at home if he or she had the patience.

The first of these small gauges was 9.5mm launched by the French firm of Pathe in 1922, at first as a home cinema outfit. A small hand-turned projector, the Pathe Baby, costing £6.15s (£6.75), soon reduced to five pounds, was available and with a 12 volt lamp running off the domestic electricity supply, a three-foot picture was obtainable over a twelve-foot throw. Short printed-down versions of cinema films could be purchased outright. Subjects included natural history, sport, comedies and cartoons. These came in metal cassettes that slotted into the projector and contained 30ft or 60ft of film.

The Pathe Baby was a well-made machine and many hundreds of thousands were produced over the following ten years. It contained one most ingenious device. A notch, a small area of the film clipped out, on the right hand side of a frame, activated a freeze frame mechanism in the projector. This held the notched frame still in the projector gate for about seven seconds, after which the mechanism returned automatically to normal projection. With this device titles could be printed for a frame or two only. Static scenes which contained no movement, could also be notched. This saved valuable film time, therefore the one and a quarter minute running time of a 30ft cassette could be considerably increased with the aid of notches. Pathe's novel notching idea lasted into the mid-1930s, until brighter pictures were demanded. The hotter lamps burnt the notched frame that stood in the gate of the

Accessories could be added to the 9.5 Pathe Baby projector. This one has spool arms to enable longer films to be shown and an electric motor drive.

projector, so the technique was eventually abandoned. In 1923 a beautifully made camera for 9.5mm was put on the market. Measuring only four inches high, 3½ inches long and 1½ inches wide, this hand-operated machine was best used on a tripod. The handle was turned at two revolutions per second on the screen. Pathe worked out this was the slowest rate required to produce a non-flickering picture. It wasn't long however before sixteen frames per second became the standard speed of amateur cameras - a rate borrowed from the 35mm standard size of the cinema.

The Pathe Baby camera held a daylight loading cassette of 30ft of film. Each cost 3s.4d (16p), but cheaper reloads were available. A further 2s. (10p) paid for development. About 1927 Pathe started supplying attachments for the projector so that longer films could be shown, and about the same time the first of a series of clockwork-driven movie cameras appeared. Right from the time 9.5mm was marketed seriously in this country, from about 1925, the system was extremely popular with the amateur movement. The equipment was cheap, and so was the film. Family films are often just as important as documentaries. Films of seaside

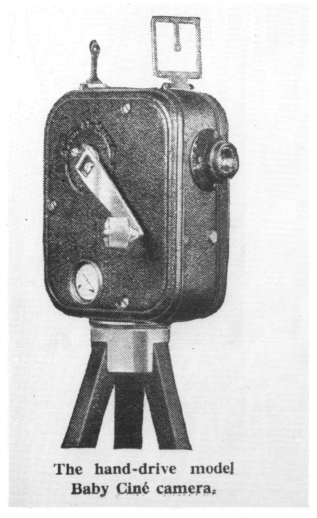

The hand-drive model
Baby Ciné camera.

Above: The hand-turned Pathe Baby 9.5 camera which sold for £5. A powerful spring motor drive could be attached for an additional two guineas.

holidays, babies on the lawn and weddings all help to add to the picture of how we used to live and play. A film may be short, only a minute or so; it may even be notched. In 1931 the wedding of Frederick Ward and Madge Billington was filmed at Fen Ditton church on two cassettes of 9.5mm. In this short film we see the guests, bridesmaids, the groom, the bride and best man arriving and walking up the church path. After the ceremony Mr.and Mrs.Ward emerge from the church in a shower of confetti,walk to a waiting car and drive off. Brief as it is, this film of a family wedding is wonderfully evocative of the period and of the gauge.9.5mm was the backbone of the many cine societies that came into being at this time. In East Anglia there was the Cambridge Photographic Club Cineworkers, Norwich Amateur Cine Society, See All Film Society (Loughton, Essex), Felixstowe Amateur Productions and Colchester Cine Club. The last-named, with Sidney Mann as the driving

Scenes from the 1931 wedding of Frederick Ward and Madge Billington at Fen Ditton Church. Note the notch, the cut-out area on the right hand side of the picture on the frame of the guests walking up the church path which held the frame stationary in the projector so that the audience had a longer look at their friends.

Colchester Cine Club projection team at a public show. Left to right: Colin Noon, John Jones, David Lewis.

force, had no connection with the present Colchester Cine Club, which was founded in 1959. This club today has some very active members and a catalogue of over 50 films of Colchester and the immediate area. The Norwich Amateur Cine Society, formed in 1933, met in Bacon House in Colegate where the owner's collection of antiques and period furniture was allowed to be used in the films. The president of the club was local cinema owner and film enthusiast Victor Harrison.

Other film societies that got going in the early Thirties were Lowestoft Secondary School Cine Club, Southend-on-Sea Amateur Film Society, Newmarket Amateur Cine Society and West Essex Film Society, who made one film on 35mm. The use of 35mm by amateurs was not unusual. Anthony Buxton of Horsey Hall in East Norfolk was making 35mm films of bird life on the Norfolk Broads in the 1930s, and Cambridge University Film Society also used this gauge to record the building of the new University Library in 1933. Cambridge students were busy again about 1962

Below: Members of the Norwich Cine Club not long after it was founded.

with a fictional film, "A Shilling Life", again on 35mm, about an unhappy undergraduate recently arrived in the town.

Kodak's 8mm, launched in 1932, grew steadily in popularity, partly due to the excellent quality of Kodachrome colour film marketed in the mid 1930s. After the Second World War 8mm overtook 9.5mm which had mainly been supported by the British company that first promoted it, Pathescope. Pathescope ceased trading in 1960, and 9.5mm is now an obsolete gauge. In the 1960s Kodak redesigned 8mm film to give an increased picture area for better quality. Super 8mm, as it is called, was launched in 1965.

Kodak's 16mm is a success story. Used extensively in television, education and the commercial and sponsored film world, 16mm first appeared in 1923 as a complete movie-making outfit. "It opens wide the door to personal motion pictures", said Kodak. Right from the start it was used by the more serious amateur film makers because it gave better quality than 9.5mm and the cameras held 100ft of film, enough for four minutes' filming. Kodak's first 16mm camera, the Cine Kodak A, was hand turned, cumbersome and not very successful, one reason being that the viewfinder not only reversed the image so that the picture appeared the wrong way round but presented it upside down as well. In 1926 the first of a long line of good quality and robust 16mm cameras, the Kodak B, appeared. A hundred-foot roll of 16mm film cost 30s (£1.50), including processing. The Kodak B could be bought for 16 guineas (£16.80) and a projector, the Kodascope A, for £40. This, Kodak said, was capable of projecting a picture twelve feet wide - an enormous magnification for a frame 10mm wide and 7½mm high. The next projector that came out was the Kodascope B, a luxurious machine that threaded the film itself. It cost £89.50, a lot of money in the 1920s. A cheaper manual model was then marketed, the Kodascope C, for £15.

Luckily many East Anglians, like Barrett Jenkins, of Southwold, used this gauge to make films of local subjects which they could show to audiences outside the home. Barrett Jenkins' father, Frederick Jenkins, was a photographer with a shop in Southwold High Street which sold stationery, artist's materials, hand-made pottery, gramophones, wirelesses and photographic materials. Barrett, then in his twenties, worked in the shop. In 1928 a Kodak BB cine camera (a smaller version of the B) came into the shop, but it never had the chance of being bought by a customer, for Barrett took it from the shelves, grabbed some film from the same place and started recording local events.

Above: The four main gauges of film in their silent form. From left to right: Standard 8mm, 9.5 mm, 16mm and 35mm.

Left: A Kodak BB 16mm camera. This version held fifty foot of film enough for two minutes of filming. This camera, now in the Archive Museum, belonged to Barrett Jenkins of Southwold.

Southwold Station during the last week of operation in 1929. Barrett Jenkins is seen on the right hand side of the group with his 16mm movie camera.

On 28th May 1928, Whit Monday, Barrett filmed the races and prizegiving of the Rural Sports, held on the common. These sports had flourished before the First World War, and this was an attempt to revive them. Although on the film everyone seemed to be enjoying themselves, these Rural Sports were not held again. Barrett Jenkins filmed many events in Southwold over the years including the Beating of the Bounds ceremony, Trinity Fair, and the passing of the Southwold Railway.

Photography ran in the Jenkins family. Henry Jenkins, 1838-1921, was a photographer in Tunbridge Wells who had 14 children, six of whom became photographers. Of those six Annie Jenkins went to Worthing, Ernest to Redhill and Polly to Cape Town. Samuel Jenkins stayed in Tunbridge Wells, Frederick Jenkins set up in business in Southwold and Harry in Lowestoft. Harry's son Ford Jenkins was well known for his photographs of the fishing fleets at Lowestoft, and in 1930 he made "Herring Fisheries", a fifteen-minute film very much like "Drifters". He was probably influenced by Grierson's film, as he did

see it around this time, although he could not remember exactly when.

"Herring Fisheries" follows the "Drifters" pattern. The boats leave harbour and the nets are cast; numerous shots of hauling follow with some interesting camera angles and quick cutting. Back at Lowestoft the catch is landed and the fish gutted. There are shots of barrelling and boxing the herring and finally we see crates for export being loaded into the hold of a steamer.

It is a well made film with captions explaining the procedures and equipment, but like John Grierson, Ford Jenkins had trouble in obtaining the fishing shots he wanted. It was the practice of the herring drifters to go to sea one day and to return the next morning, but if the catch was poor they would stay at sea another night or so.

Armed with his 16mm camera and a supply of film, Ford Jenkins went to sea in a Lowestoft drifter one autumn afternoon. At seven the next morning the crew began hauling in the two miles of net. There was not a single fish in it. The drifter

Above: A frame from Ford Jenkin's film of the herring fisheries at Lowestoft.

stayed at sea. The next night a quantity of herrings were hauled in, but all before there was any daylight to allow Ford to film. The drifter stayed at sea. The third morning produced a good catch, and Ford Jenkins was able to capture some scenes as the last nets came aboard in early daylight. The drifter returned to Lowestoft, but Ford Jenkins was not happy with the shots he had, so eventually he went to sea again - this time obtaining the results he wanted in one go.

In 1931 Ford Jenkins took his finished film to London to show to Kodak. They were so impressed they put it in the Kodascope library under the title "A Glimpse of the East Coast Herring Industry". A write-up of the film and a picture of Ford Jenkins appeared in the Cine Kodak and Kodascope Library News of August, 1931. Another version of his film was put out by Home Movies and Home Talkies, a monthly magazine for cine enthusiasts of the time under the title "North Sea Herring Harvest". But

Below: Hauling the nets - a challenge for Ford Jenkins to provide steady pictures as the drifter rolled!

this was not Ford Jenkins' first or only film. A year or so earlier he had gone out in a Hull trawler to make "A Trawling Voyage to Bear Island, Spitzbergen" on 9.5mm and later he was working on a film of the Norfolk Broads in winter.

He died in August, 1983, but his photographs and films live on. The shop overlooking the harbour (he had moved there from the original shop at 2 Pier Terrace, south of Lowestoft Bridge, in the 1950s) is now run by his son, Peter Jenkins. Outside the shop is a huge, eye-catching photograph of a Lowestoft fisherman taken by Harry Jenkins; at the old fisherman's feet are two young children, Waveney and Ford Jenkins.

Many towns in East Anglia have had their events, ceremonies and visits by Royal and important people recorded on film by enthusiastic inhabitants. For over forty years this was done in Norwich by Charles Scott.

Above: Charles Scott on one of his filming expeditions.

Cine photography began for Charles Scott in 1933, when he bought a second-hand 16mm camera for £9/9s (£9.45). Over the years he made family films, travel films, comic films and a series of films recording happenings in and around the city. His compilation "It Happened in Norwich" covered events from 1933 to 1946, including an Armistice Day parade, laying wreaths on Nurse Cavell's grave, the 1935 Jubilee celebrations, an

Men of the Home Guard manning an anti-tank mortar.

The Home Guard in Kings Lynn on parade.

F.A. Cup-Tie between Norwich and Chelsea, the 1937 Coronation procession, A.R.P. practice in 1938, the 1946 Battle of Britain Week and a Mr.Way demonstrating a model electric train around a track in his garden. In 1948 Charles Scott recorded the Whit Monday Fete in Eaton Park and a year later the dedication of the Norwich Memorial at the Cemetery in Farrow Road to Blitz victims.

Charles Scott worked as a van driver for W.& R.Jacob, the biscuit makers. During the war when petrol became hard to find the biscuit companies formed a delivery pool, all the different companies, Huntley and Palmers, Peek Freans, Westons, Macfarlane Langs, Kemps and Jacobs combining their distribution. A depot was set up at King's Lynn, close to the railway station, and Charles Scott spent the rest of the war years there as manager. The temptation to make films was great, but unexposed cine film was hard to come by in wartime.

Charles had joined the Home Guard in Lynn, and one Sunday with just 50 feet of film in the camera he recorded uniformed members on guard at the Cut Bridge over the Ouse near Lynn. When he showed the film to his comrades they were "thrilled" and wanted a longer film made. An officer managed to obtain film, with the proviso that it was used for an instructional film about the Home Guard.

Charles Scott set to work. He recreated the formation of the Local Defence Volunteers, as the Home Guard was first known, following the broadcast on May 14th, 1940, by Anthony Eden asking for people of the country to come forward to form an internal countrywide army. For a silent film the broadcast was ingeniuously covered. First there is a title giving the date, then a shot of a clock

coming up to 9 p.m. Next comes a shot of a radio, followed by pictures on the front covers of two magazines, showing Kitchener pointing (everyone knew the famous First World War poster of Lord Kitchener pointing out of the picture at the viewer saying "Your country needs you") and Anthony Eden, Secretary of State for War.

With long shots, close ups, low angles and tracking shots, Charles Scott filmed volunteers being kitted out, attending lectures, and at drill practice. The men of Number 2 Platoon, 3 Company, 7th Battalion, Norfolk Home Guard co-operated fully with their filming colleague. In fact Charles Scott recorded their activities right up to 1945, when they attended their last parade in the Tuesday Market Place at Lynn.

After the war, Charles Scott returned to Norwich and to filming. He filmed the erection of the prefabricated houses made in aeroplane factories to replace houses demolished in air raids, the rebuilding of Curls Store (later Debenhams) on the bombed site in Orford Place, and in 1951 the Norwich celebrations of the Festival of Britain. In 1979, at the age of 79, Charles Scott purchased an 8mm camera and projector, laying aside the 16mm camera that had served him for 46 years.

During the 1930s a very unusual film was made showing the work of the Mutual Service Clubs in Norwich after a Church of England organisation, the Industrial Christian Fellowship, had looked into the problem of mass unemployment in the city. The outcome was the setting up of the Norwich Unemployment Welfare Association by Oliver Findlow, who also became its organiser. The aim was to help the unemployed avoid bitterness and disillusionment, and to create opportunities for mutual participation, rather than

Above: A tailor helped to repair clothes which the unemployed could then buy cheaply.

Scenes from Charles Scott's film of a prefab being put together in the Dereham Road area of Norwich. He covered both the erection of the buildings, and the occupants moving in and undertaking an essential task!

just doing things for them. Open air meetings were held in Norwich Market Place, where many of the unemployed men tended to congregate, to find out how best to help.

What the men wanted was somewhere to go, a rest room or the like. The City Council was approached and a room in a disused and dilapidated factory on the site of the present City Hall was offered, with materials for the men to do it up. Oliver Findlow now came up against the first problem. The men refused to work, claiming that it would be scab labour, unless they were paid full trade union rates for the job. Oliver Findlow recorded having "two or three very unpleasant meetings" but eventually the problem was sorted out. Tables and forms and a tea urn were loaned, and the first Mutual Service Club, as it was known, was under way.

But the rest room was inadequate. Much bigger premises were required, if Oliver Findlow's plans were to be brought to fruition, so a three-storeyed house in Pottergate Street belonging to one of the Colmans was rented for a shilling a year, and the aims of the Norwich Unemployment Welfare Association were put into practice. These aims were to stimulate and encourage a sense of comradeship, to encourage men to regain and retain craftsmanship, to promote, by lectures and discussions, an interest in the affairs of life, to provide facilities for indoor and outdoor recreations and sport and to advise and help in all cases of need. The new club in Pottergate consisted of offices, a games room, a canteen, a room for the blind, concert and lecture rooms, a quiet room which also served as a chapel, library and workshops.

A number of schemes for the men were put into operation. There was the Allotment Scheme which, with the help of the City Parks Department providing three hundred plots, enabled the men to grow enough food to feed a family for a year for an outlay of about twelve shillings (60 pence) for seeds and tools. The allotments were rent free.

There was a carpentry shop where the men could build anything from a child's toy to a garden shed. But nothing could be sold. The men only paid for the materials they used. Old boots and shoes were given by the people of Norwich and under the expert guidance of a shoe maker, the men repaired these for their own and family use, using leather off-cuts given by a local shoe factory. There was a similar scheme for clothes. Outdoors there were cricket, football and bowls teams, and inside billiards, chess, draughts, cards and bagatelle games. There was even a club for unemployed women and girls. District clubs were set up at Lakenham, Thorpe, Heigham, Mile Cross and New Costessey. Between 1932 and 1939 these Mutual Service Clubs dealt with over thirty thousand men and women, all of whom were interviewed by the founder, Oliver Findlow. On 29th October, 1938, the King and Queen visited the club while in Norwich to open the City Hall.

During 1938 a 16mm film shot by Mr Harvey of Coes was made showing all aspects of the club's work, culminating with the Royal Visit. ''Time on their Hands'', a thirty-minute silent film paid for by one of the Friends, is all that exists now of a forgotten piece of social work of the 1930s, which succeeded because of its enthusiastic and tireless Industrial Christian Fellowship organiser, Oliver C.Findlow.

In Ipswich, Don Chipperfield has been making films for over fifty years. He started in 1928 with a 9.5mm camera, but in 1933, after joining Ransomes, Sims and Jefferies, he was helping to film their trolley buses around the town on 16mm.

Trolley buses, collecting electricity from overhead wires, ran in Ipswich for 40 years, ending in 1963. Many were made in Ransomes' Orwell Works, close to the docks, and in 1935, when Ransomes received an order for fifty trolley buses for Cape Town, a record was made in great detail of the building of an electric trolley bus. This was the beginning of a life of film making. Don Chipperfield also made comedies and dramas with Ransomes' Social Club members and newsreels of their events. In 1935 he was a founder member of the Ipswich Film Society, which was among the first in the provinces. Basil Wright, Edgar Anstey and Alberto Cavalcanti were just a few of the famous film makers of the time who came to Ipswich to

Don Chipperfield filming at Nacton for Ransomes in the 1970's

Trolley buses in Ipswich in 1934, one of Don Chipperfield's early films.

Ben Whiting, the last rope maker of Hadleigh in Suffolk.

speak to the society. In 1985, a thousand feature films later, the society celebrated its 50th anniversary.

In 1950 Don Chipperfield began producing publicity and advertising films for Ransomes and a film library was set up. Films on agricultural and grass machinery and instructional films dealing with ploughing, spraying and harvesting were made. "Speed the Plough", made in the early 1950s, shows a day in the life of the agricultural machinery shop. Men arrive at work, machines start up and the foundry begins pouring molten metal. The production lines for assembling ploughs, cultivators, disc harrows and potato lifters are seen in the Victorian atmosphere of Orwell Works. The construction of a heavy trailer plough is followed through in detail from the bending of the steel beam which forms the backbone of the plough to the paint shop, until the finished plough leaves the factory in gleaming condition. In 1977 Don Chipperfield was in charge of a number of local cameramen recording the Queen's visit to Ipswich as part of her travels around Britain in Jubilee year. Film making is Don Chipperfield's passion in life and in the last fifty years it has taken him all over the world. "There was hardly ever a dull moment", he says, seventy countries and 84 miles of film later.

The filming of local crafts, industries and manufacturing processes in the Hadleigh area began in 1946 when Peter Boulton and Gilbert Hawker set up Boulton Hawker Films, whose main objective was to make educational films. One of the first was "Rope Making by Hand", demonstrated by Ben Whiting and filmed in Pound Lane, Hadleigh. Mr Whiting, who had been making rope in a traditional way for sixty years, walks backwards, feeding out through his fingers the sisal, the fluffy spun yarn which is festooned around his middle.

The other end is fastened to "whirls", small revolving wheels that twist the sisal as the rope-maker backs away. Three of these strands would then be twisted together, again using whirls to form a rope. Making rope in this way on a rope-walk was a very ancient craft, although it continued at Haverhill into the 1970s. Other educational films made by Boulton Hawker in these early years show how coconut matting was made in the Brett works of E.H.Price at Hadleigh, and the process of malting at Wilson's maltings in the same town. Films on agriculture, market gardening and geography have been made, but some extra income for the business was obtained from distributing other people's films, both in this country and abroad. The main income, however, came from the Educational Foundation for Visual Aids set up in 1948 to co-ordinate production and provide financial help for educational film makers in the form of a guaranteed final order for 12 copies of each film made with a teacher advisor appointed by them. This went on until the late 1970s when cuts in education rendered it impossible to continue. Gilbert Hawker left in the 1950s to work on his own in Ipswich. One of the films he made then showed how the Ipswich Evening Star was produced, from the selection of a story, through printing, to the finished newspaper being sold by newsboys. Gilbert Hawker also made films for the Ipswich engineering firm of Ransomes and Rapier. Boulton Hawker films continue under the guidance of Peter Boulton who has seen great changes in the use of film for education over the years. Movie films in blacked-out classrooms are almost a thing of the past. Today the video machine rules, but films are produced with the overseas market in mind, in particular the U.S.A. Thus Boulton-Hawker works with American as well as British advisors; the overseas market representing about 95% of income.

Above: Eric Stevenson at work in his Wroxham forge in Peter Hollingham's film "The Blacksmith".

Above: Making flower-pots by hand at Upshire in Essex.

In Essex and Norfolk, the education authorities organised large libraries of cine film for distribution to schools. These libraries are still in existence, but videotape has almost completely taken over as the medium for reproduction of educational material. Most of these library films were bought in, but both the Visual and Aural Aids Service in Chelmsford and the Visual Aids Section in Norwich made films of their own.

In the early 1950s, the county film service of Essex produced a series of films on a wide range of subjects. "Country Manners", 1952, dealt with litter in the countryside and the havoc it could cause; "Witness in Brass" looked at the way to make brass rubbings and showed how to make a positive copy from the original, and "Safety Line", 1956, records the maintenance of electric trains at Ilford.

There were also some films showing how things were made. "Flower Pots", filmed at the potteries of G. & A. Tuck Ltd. at Upshire, Waltham Abbey, in 1954, looks at techniques used in an industry which was combining up to date and traditional methods. It shows pots being moulded by mechanical presses, as well as those being thrown on a wheel by craftsmen. It also shows modern earth-moving equipment digging out the clay, which is then left to weather, just as it had been for centuries in such a traditional industry. Both the pugmill in which the clay is ground and mixed and the coal-fuelled down-draught kiln where the pots are fired are illustrated by animated diagrams as well as in reality.

Other films in the series show glass bottles being made at the Key Glass Works at Harlow, and cricket bats at Little Baddow in 1958.

Some films from the Essex Library were made as

part of a course on cinematography at Wansfell, a residential adult college at Theydon Bois, in the early 1950s. William Cottis and Sons foundry at Epping is the subject of "Iron Foundry", in which the making of small agricultural equipment is shown in detail, and the production of the West Essex Gazette is followed in "Local Newspaper", which shows the whole process from the writing of the story by a reporter to the setting out of the page using hot metal "slugs" cast on a Linotype machine and the printing of the newspaper on a rotary letterpress machine. This system is increasingly being replaced by offset lithography and photosetting techniques.

Peter Hollingham has been making films for the Media Resources Centre, as the visual aids section of Norfolk Education Service is now known, for 25 years. He travels all over Norfolk from his base in Witard Road, Norwich and like his colleagues at Chelmsford he now takes out video equipment to record crafts and industries of the area for use in Norfolk schools. In 1977, while still working with 16mm film, Peter Hollingham filmed master blacksmith Eric Stevenson.

Eric Stevenson, B.E.M. (an award received for organising local fire-fighting units in the Second World War) retired in 1977 after forty-nine years at his Wroxham forge, where Stevensons had been working since 1815. Farm implements, boat work, weather vanes and village signs were all part of his job, though he specialised in church and cathedral work. In 1977 he restored the gates of London's St. Paul's Cathedral, made by Jean Tijoue in the 17th century. Eric Stevenson has a copy of the original bill dated August 29th, 1699. "For the great gates on the outside of the church, leading to the east side of the south portico and a wicket in the middle of it, framed with strong iron and ornaments with points - £160."

The gates, valued at £8,000 in 1977, were badly rusted and Eric Stevenson had to replace parts with fresh wrought iron. In "The Blacksmith" he shows the gates to a party of schoolchildren visiting his forge in Norwich Road, Wroxham. He talks about his work and describes to his young visitors how he would make a scroll or join two pieces together.

Peter Hollingham's film then moves to St. Nicholas' Church at Great Yarmouth, where details of the screen, more of Eric Stevenson's work, are shown in close-up. He made the five screens weighing fifteen tons over a six-year period from 1963 to 1969, and at the same time he made his own 8mm film of the work.

Even in these days of video there are still film makers working on 8mm and 16mm throughout East Anglia. Paul Amos of Dovercourt is as keen now as he was in 1953 when he first started making 9.5mm films of events and happenings in his native area with a Pathescope Pat -a simple 9.5mm camera launched in Coronation Year. Now he uses a Bolex H16, a high quality 16mm camera, and Kodachrome movie film to record anything of interest, whether it is topical like the Redoubt Fete at Harwich or historical like the restoration of Harwich Electric Palace Cinema. At Haughley Geoffrey Clarke is the village recorder, and using both 16mm and 8mm makes regular "newsreels" of happenings in the vicinity. These and other film makers keep up the tradition.

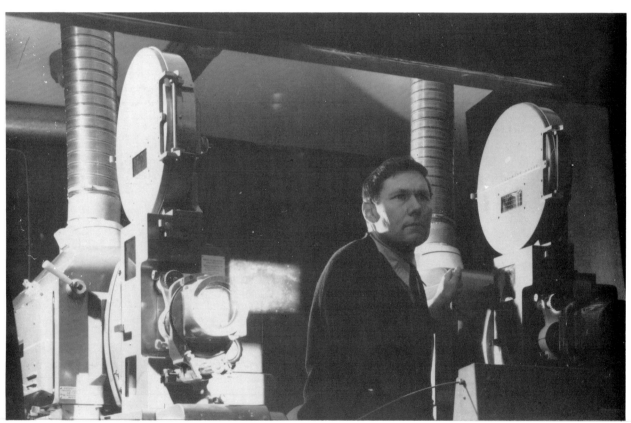

Paul Amos operating a 35mm projector at the University of Essex.

Saving the Past

The idea of keeping films for historical evidence is not new. Robert Paul, a pioneer film maker, suggested it in the 1890s, and in 1906 someone proposed that "bioscopical records" should be deposited in the British Museum. Frederick Talbot, writing in "Moving Pictures, how they are made and worked" in 1912, said "the suggestion has been made that records of the most important events of today, such as the Coronation of King George V, the unveiling of the Victoria Memorial, the Durbar, and so forth, should be preserved in a museum for the benefit of generations a century or more hence. Impressions of the voices of our greatest singers are being preserved for posterity, and the question has been asked why historical cinematographic films should not be treated in the same manner." It took another twenty years before the subject was tackled seriously enough for a national archive to be set up.

The newsreel companies were conscious of what they were recording and were keeping their films, even if they had an eye on the commercial outlook. "The Pathe Gazette records history as it happens; it preserves for the future great men and their deeds" ran an advertisement in 1920. In fact, Pathe did just as they said; although they no longer make newsreels, the Pathe Library is still in existence, an Aladdin's cave for the television producer who wants archive film for his programme.

The National Film Archive was formed in 1935. Originally called the National Film Library, it has over the years built up a most impressive collection of films covering every aspect of the cinema.

But one thing the N.F.A. has not been able to cover is local history. This is where the regional film archives come in. In April, 1976, the author, then of the Educational Technology Unit at the University of Essex, attended the British Universities Film Council conference at Southampton. One of the subjects discussed was the use of archive newsreel film for educational purposes and his report of the conference suggested that a collection of locally made films should be started. David Tilley, Director of the E.T.U. at the time, together with the author, approached Malcolm Freegard, Director of the Audio-Visual Centre at the University of East Anglia, who had similar ideas. Between them they set up the East Anglian Film Archive and after a busy few months a nucleus of film had been gathered. Right from the start, the Eastern Arts Association provided the bulk of the money needed for the job of preserving films, and this resulted in

the film archive's area being drawn up - Norfolk, Suffolk, Essex and Cambridgeshire. The help of Eastern Arts enabled the first compilation film to be made by the archive in June 1976, bringing together James Blyth's local newsreels of Southwold into a film entitled "Southwold, Past and Present". In the same month television raided the archive's small collection for the first time.

Two other regional archives came into being around this time. Inheriting an existing collection from the Scottish Film Council, the Scottish Film Archive was established in November, 1976, with Janet McBain as archivist, and in June, 1977, the North-West Film Archive was formed. Under the guidance of Seona Robertson and Maryann Gomes, this archive has steadily built up a collection of films of the Manchester area.

Above: The catalogue of the East Anglian Film Archive, which can be purchased from the Archive at the University of East Anglia.

These regional archives were set up quite independently of one another. All had the same job to do, to search out non-fiction film of local interest, to preserve it for the future, and as far as copyright allows, to let as many people as possible see it. After all, movie film was made to be seen, not to be stored away for ever in a can. During the first ten years of the East Anglian Film Archive more than 840 lecture film shows were presented by members of the Archive throughout East Anglia from Cromer to Southend, from Lowestoft to Peterborough.

Since 1979 the East Anglian Film Archive has been housed at the University of East Anglia in Norwich, where it is run jointly by the Audio-Visual Centre and the Centre of East Anglian Studies. Here there is a small museum of cine equipment, mostly donated by film enthusiasts in the region, air-conditioned vaults for the master negatives and positives, and a viewing room.

The cost of running a film archive is high. There are filing systems to be prepared, catalogues to be printed, equipment to be bought -but these are small items compared with the film itself. It can cost over £1,000 to save one thirty-minute film. The main income from the Eastern Arts Association is supplement by smaller grants from firms and councils in the Archive's region.

But in a hundred, two hundred or even three hundred years' time the money spent now will seem insignificant against the images that have been saved, showing how we lived, worked and played. Who knows, by the twenty-second century there may be another method of storing and recording moving pictures. We must do our job now to make sure that future generations at least have the opportunity to view the past and possibly to preserve it for another three hundred years.

Preserving moving pictures is not an easy business. One of the greatest problems is, as Frederick Talbot realised in 1912,"the perishable character of celluloid film". Not long ago all 35mm gauge film distributed to cinemas was on nitrate stock. Nitrate - or more correctly cellulose nitrate, commonly called celluloid - was manufactured by Kodak until 1951; other manufacturers ceased production soon afterwards. Nitrate film continued to circulate in cinemas until the late 1950s, although by that time the distributors had inserted a notice in the leaders of the film informing the projectionist it was a nitrate print. Nitrate film is highly inflammable and has a built-in decomposition rate which eventually destroys the film and its image. Careful storage can slow down this process, but eventually everything worth saving has to be copied on to modern safety stock - which is reckoned to last for two to three hundred years.

It is surprising how much nitrate film there is about. Small collections continue to come to light in record offices, libraries, town hall vaults, garages, cellars and lofts, storage places which are seldom conducive to keeping the film and its image in good condition. Fluctuating temperatures and dampness are the enemies of celluloid. The picture begins to fade and the film becomes sticky, the emulsion peels off as the film is unwound, and slowly the film becomes a solid mass, eventually turning to brown powder. By the time the stickiness is first noticed it is already almost too late, so it is important that nitrate film should be copied as soon as it is found. The smaller gauges of 8mm, 9.5mm and 16mm do not suffer from this problem as they were designed for use with non-inflammable safety stock - which does not decompose - right from the start to make them more suitable for home use.

But whatever the original gauge, the film has to be compatible with modern requirements. 16mm is the most versatile size at present, so the working gauge of the East Anglian Film Archive's viewing collection is 16mm. 35mm films are preserved on 35mm to keep the quality and 16mm reduction prints made for normal viewing. Both 8mm and 9.5mm are "blown-up" to the 16mm gauge in either negative or positive form and a viewing print

Above: Sound versions of the four gauges of film. Left to right: Super 8mm, with a magnetic sound-track down the right hand side. The other films have optical sound tracks. 9.5 and 35mm had their picture areas reduced to accommodate the sound track.

Below: Decomposing 35mm film. The film is solid and the picture has disappeared.

Above: Nitrate film that has suffered badly from damp.

Below: Film safely copied and stored at the East Anglian Film Archive.

made. This is the principle of all archives - to keep the original or a duplicate of it under the best possible conditions - the preservation collection being used solely for making viewing copies when required.

Videotape is used increasingly for viewing purposes, but it is not a preservation medium. Video is at present restricted to the small screen, often destroying the original feeling of the film, which was intended for large screen presentation.

Television is now the great recorder of East Anglian life and a wealth of material exists on film in the television archives, both in the region and outside. Unfortunately, none of this is available in a more permanent form for the people who want to see it and have paid for it - either directly by the licence fee or indirectly by buying goods that finance advertising.

Television came to East Anglia in 1959 when the BBC opened a regional station at Norwich three weeks ahead of the Independent Television Authority's franchise holder for the area, Anglia Television. The first programme from the BBC was broadcast on October 5th when Geoffrey Harvey read the news in a hastily equipped studio in St. Catherine's Close - the same building that BBC East occupies today. This programme, soon to be known as "East at Six Ten" (each word so arranged on the screen that EAST was formed down the left hand side of the picture) was the fore-runner of "Look East".

The BBC had taken over St.Catherine's Close in 1956 to make local radio programmes that were inserted into the Midland Home Service via the new VHF transmitter at Tacolneston. This transmitter was then used to bring the main BBC television programmes to East Anglia.

Above: St. Catherine's Close, the home of the BBC in Norwich since 1956.

Above: David Kenten and cameraman shooting for the "Bygones" programme. (Photo: Anglia Television)

The 1960 feature series programmes from BBC television in Norwich were "Farming Club" produced by Gordon Mosley and "Outlook", a magazine programme produced by Malcolm Freegard which reflected the life of the region and delved into the lores and legends of the area during its two-year run. A good deal of local history was recorded on film by these and other programmes, only a fraction of which survives.

Anglia Television, through reports in "About Anglia" and in feature programmes, has built up the most comprehensive film library of East Anglian life of the 1960s and 1970s, with subjects recorded just before they disappeared into the past, such as the workings of the old Norwich City Library in Charing Cross, before the move to Bethel Street, and the running of the last trolley-buses in Ipswich in 1963. There is "The Craftsmen" series with such people as thatcher Eric Cutting and Wickham Market miller Edward Rackham. Major features of the 1970s include "No Lullaby for Broadland", chronicling the problems of the Broads, and "Gone

to Burton", the story of the farmworkers' migration in the early part of this century to Burton-on-Trent in the winter months to find work in the malting houses.

Anglia Television's longest running programmes have been "Farming Diary" (1959) and "About Anglia" (1960), both introduced in the early days by Norfolk farmer Dick Joice. With his enthusiasm for country matters and the past, Dick Joice and his producer David Kenten (who has a nose for unearthing archive film himself) have recorded much valuable material on film over the years in documentaries, "Bygones Specials" and "Bygones" itself.

Much of the technical work of making these films is carried on in the building in which Anglia first started in 1959, formerly the Agricultural Hall. It was in that same building that the films of Birt Acres, one of the first people to operate a movie camera in this country, were presented by Gilbert's Modern Circus on January 11th, 1897.

LLOYD'S NEWS ☞

SONG-PICTURES and
BIOSCOPE ✳ ✳
ENTERTAINMENT.

Some East Anglian Press Opinions.

East Anglian Daily Times.

On Tuesday evening, the proprietors of the "Daily Chronicle" and "Lloyd's News" gave an excellent entertainment in the Co-operative Hall at Wickham Market, which was well attended. The various items were selections on the gramophone and a fine selection of animated pictures, including a striking series entitled, "From Forest to Fireside," showing the making of paper, printing, and delivery of a newspaper. The vocal and instrumental parts were sustained very efficiently by Mr. C. W. Wade and Miss Cissie Harcourt, and recitals by Miss Laura Godfree.

Essex and Suffolk News.

At the Victoria Hall, Sudbury, on Friday and Saturday evenings an excellent entertainment was given under the auspices of Messrs. Lloyd Ltd., the proprietors of "Lloyd's Weekly News" and the "Daily Chronicle" It consisted of "Song pictures" illustrated songs, dramatic recitals and a bioscope display, illustrating production of "Lloyd's Weekly News." It was a really enjoyable entertainment of high-class character. The song pictures were novel and very well done, Mr. T. Wade, who has a well trained baritone voice sang in spirited fashion some sailor songs. Miss Cissie Harcourt gave vivacious renderings of some charming songs which were well received. Miss Laura Godfree is an elocutionist of ability and her humorous recitations proved very acceptable. There were some capital gramaphone solos of popular artists and an amusing bioscope display. The entertainment concluded with a most interesting account of the production of "Lloyd's Weekly News," entitled "From Forest to Fireside." The lecturette was given by Mr. Alexander M. Nicol, the manager of the entertainment and there were some capital animated films of the manufacture of the pulp in Norway, the paper making mills at Sittingbourne, the largest in the world, and the printing of the paper in Fleet Street,

"Lloyds' News" has a circulation of 1,300,000 copies a week, and one machine printed them at the rate of 48,000 an hour. Mr. Nicol gave a few particulars of "Lloyds' News" scheme for the encouragement of small holders and allotment holders.

Ipswich Observer.

On Friday evening last week, a splendid entertainment arranged by the proprietors of "Lloyd's Weekly News" and the "Daily Chronicle" was given at the Lecture Hall, Ipswich. A most popular programme had been drawn up comprising illustrated songs by London vocalists, choice gramophone selections, dramatic and humourous recitals and a fine bioscope display.

Stowmarket Post.

An entertainent of a pleasingly varied type was given at the Institute, Stowmarket, on Monday evening described as "Song Pictures." Quite the feature of the evening, from a vocal point of view, was the singing of Mr. C. W. Wade the possessor of a baritone voice of exceptional excellence, and his efforts were appreciated by all. Miss Cissie Harcourt also sang well, and Miss Laura Godfree exhibited cleverness in her monologue sketch. Novel items were heard when the gramophone reproduced the efforts of such celebrated vocalists as Madame Tetrazzini and Mr. Andrew Black, these being accompanied with lantern illustrations. Altogether a very pleasant evening was spent.

Diss Reporter.

An enjoyable and at the same time instructive entertainment was given in the Corn Hall, Diss, on Tuesday and Wednesday evenings, before large audiences. The affair was organised by the proprietors of "Lloyd's News," with the object of advertising this and kindred Journals, and the entertainment, which was well organised by Mr. W. B. Hughes, took the attractive form of song pictures, gramophone selections, dramatic and humourous recitals and a bioscope display. The artistes included Miss Rose Baker (of the Grand Opera Covent Garden), Miss Laura Godfree and Mr. C.W. Wade (Queen's Hall Concerts). Miss Baker, who has a very powerful and well-trained voice, was re-called for most of her songs, and among her best performances were "My Dear Soul" and "My Ships," which quite brought down the house. Mr. Wade's efforts also met with a good reception, his capital interpretation of "The Deathless Army," being followed with demonstrations of delight, and the audience heartily joined in the chorus when he sang the ever favourite "The old Folks at home." Miss Laura Godfree, who is a clever reciter, created a very favourable impression by her capital presentation of "Gabriel Grubb" (Dickens). The "Wedding Day," given on Tuesday, was by special request repeated on Wednesday, and the latter being St. Patrick's Day, she also recited "Shamus O'Brien"—a tale of the Irish Rebellion—in which pathos and humour were intermingled, which was certainly an elocutionary treat. Records of instrumental selections, and popular songs, duets, &c., including the "Death of Nelson" and "Excelsior" were reproduced from a gramophone. All the songs were illustrated with pretty dioramic effects. The bioscope display included most amusing animated pictures, which kept the audience in roars of laughter. The bioscope was also utilized for for bringing before the audience the various processes for the production of "Lloyd's Weekly News."

Index